Employment Expansion and Metropolitan Trade

Richard Victor Knight

foreword by
Eli Ginzberg

Conservation of Human Resources Studies—
Columbia University

Employment Expansion and Metropolitan Trade.

PRAEGER SPECIAL STUDIES IN U.S. ECONOMIC, SOCIAL, AND POLITICAL ISSUES

Praeger Publishers New York Washington London

Library of Congress Cataloging in Publication Data

Knight, Richard V
    Employment expansion and metropolitan trade.

    (Conservation of human resources studies)   (Praeger
special studies in U. S. economic, social, and
political issues)
    Includes bibliographical references.
    1.   United States—Commerce—Case studies.
2.   Space in economics.   3.   Manpower policy—United
States.   I.   Title.   II.   Series: Conservation of
human resources studies.
HF3007. K55   381'. 0973   73-8178

PRAEGER PUBLISHERS
111 Fourth Avenue, New York, N.Y. 10003, U.S.A.
5, Cromwell Place, London SW7 2JL, England

Published in the United States of America in 1973
by Praeger Publishers, Inc.

This report was prepared for the Manpower Administration, U.S.
Department of Labor, under research contract (Project Number
81-36-71-01) authorized by Title I of the Manpower Development
and Training Act. Since contractors performing research under
government sponsorship are encouraged to express their own
judgment freely, the report does not necessarily represent the
department's official opinion or policy. Moreover, the contractor
is solely responsible for the factual accuracy of all material
developed in the report.

The Conservation of Human Resources Project, Columbia University, is an interdisciplinary research group now in its fourth decade of working in the field of human resources and manpower. Its investigations cover a broad spectrum with primary emphasis on the role of human resources in the economic development of the United States but including also other advanced economies and the developing world. In recent years the Conservation Project has increasingly focused on metropolitan labor markets. The Project also engages in research in health policy issues. Professor Eli Ginzberg, 525 Uris, Columbia University, New York, New York 10027, is director of the Project.

ACKNOWLEDGMENTS

There are numerous individuals and organizations whose support contributed to this effort. First and foremost, I am indebted to my father, an economist with interests somewhat similar to mine, and to my mother, who provided a home base. I wish, too, to thank Professor Harry Ernst for making his Introductory Principles course in economics at Tufts College so interesting that I gave up civil engineering as my major. I would like to acknowledge the experience I gained while working for private industry in market, media, and economic research, particularly with Chuck Anderson, while at The U.S. Economics Corporation/Econometric Institute. I want to thank all the members of the Conservation of Human Resources staff—in particular, Eli Ginzberg, Tom Stanback, Harry Greenfield, Dale Hiestand, Marcia Friedman, Dean Morse, Tadek Korn, Sylvia Leaf, Charlotte Frick, and Bill Lawrence, who heard me out and helped me out whenever needed. I also want to thank members of the academic community, particularly Bernard Corry and Richard C. Estall, my tutors at The London School of Economics and Political Science, University of London, for their help and encouragement, and Leland S. Burns at University of California, Los Angeles, and William Alonso at University of California, Berkeley, for carefully reading my manuscript and for making many perceptive suggestions, only a few of which, unfortunately, I was able to incorporate into this book. I borrowed many ideas from members of the academic community, acknowledged in footnotes, but there are a few individuals whose ideas pervade this work, though they may not be identified or cited fully: I am thinking of Lewis Mumford, Arnold Toynbee, Jane Jacobs, René Dubos, Wilbur Thompson, Dick Netzer, and Eric Lampart, in particular.

The development of this study, while building on the cumulative work of many, required considerable support from the government. Two agencies deserve particular mention: the Department of Commerce (and Lowell D. Ashby, who constructed the basic data file), and the Department of Labor (and the Manpower Administration), with whom the Conservation of Human Resources Project contracted to undertake this study.

All the ideas, data files, and expenditures would have been to little avail had my wife not had the patience to teach me how to put them on the printed page. Her task was called editing, and she did it at great sacrifice to her other interests.

The development of economics can be seen as the uncoordinated elaboration of specialized theories and methodologies, each of which goes its own way until it is forced into a confrontation with another, usually as the result of pressures from the political arena. Although this generalization does not hold for all times and places—and of course it does not—it provides a useful framework within which to consider the present work by Richard Knight. We will use this framework to call attention to the origins of Knight's work, his major findings about the recent changes in metropolitan trade and employment, and the significance of his methodology and findings for manpower policy and programming.

As a member of the Conservation of Human Resources staff at Columbia University, Knight collaborated with Thomas Stanback on *The Metropolitan Economy* (New York: Columbia University Press, 1970), and his present work is an extension and refinement of this earlier approach. The Conservation Project explored related dimensions of metropolitan economies and manpower in *Manpower Strategy for the Metropolis*, Eli Ginzberg and associates (New York: Columbia University Press, 1968) and *Electronic Data Processing in New York City*, Boris Yavitz and Thomas Stanback (New York: Columbia University Press, 1967). In fact the watershed in this arena for the Conservation Project was the publication of *The Pluralistic Economy* by Eli Ginzberg, Dale L. Hiestand, and Beatrice G. Reubens (New York: McGraw-Hill, 1964), which delineated the inadequacy of the model that most economists use and argued the need for studying the dynamics of employment creation in its own terms, not as a simple derivative of macroeconomic policies.

In short, Knight's book is the most recent exemplar of an approach that the Conservation Project has been pursuing since the middle 1960s to explore employment dynamics at a disaggregate level. Stanley Friedlander's *Unemployment in the Urban Core: An Analysis of Thirty Cities with Policy Recommendations* (New York: Praeger Publishers, 1972) is part of this new approach, as is Charles Brecher's *Upgrading Blue Collar and Service Workers* (Baltimore: The Johns Hopkins Press, 1972). The Conservation staff's *New York Is Very Much Alive: A Manpower View* (New York: McGraw-Hill, 1973) develops this approach further with a focus on the New York City labor market.

While Knight was influenced by his immediate research environs, his principal intellectual ties are with a much older and well-established specialty of regional economics. A long line of able theoreticians, reinforced by competent empiricists, have been developing and refining models of regional growth. Those who are acquainted with this literature will have little difficulty in recognizing the critical concepts and approaches that Knight has adopted from the regional economists as well as the significant refinements and additions that he has made to them to probe more deeply the dynamics of metropolitan trade and employment.

Illustrative of the effectiveness with which Knight modified existing approaches and developed new ones are the following: his emphasis on the export of services in using the classic export-base hypothesis; the development of a value added per employee (VAPE) measure, which enables the author to take account of changes in income generated per employee in assessing changes in metropolitan trade and employment; the creation of another measure, geographic shift of export activity (GSEA), by which he can make an estimate of intraregional and interregional shift of employment in trade activity; and the application to metropolitan trade of an old standby in international economics, the employment terms of trade (ETOT), which helps to clarify how changes in the value added of goods exported and imported alter the position of metropolitan and non-metropolitan trading partners.

Knight's major contribution lies not in his refinement of preexisting methodology but in his far-reaching empirical investigations. Multitudinous calculations underlie his systematic analysis of the exports and imports of 368 metropolitan areas during two decades, 1940-50 and 1950-60. Moreover, he studied two further dimensions of these metropolitan areas: their relations to non-metropolitan areas and their role in the context of regional development. It is a rare investigator who shows strength on all three fronts—conceptualization, methodology, and empirical analysis.

Since Knight has summarized his major findings in the concluding chapter of his book, we will limit our consideration here to a selected few that will help demonstrate the implications of his work for manpower policy and programming.

During the two decades 1940 to 1960, all metropolitan areas grew to meet increased local needs resulting from larger numbers of people and more income per capita. A closer look at the two decades reveals disparate movements among the cities, but the basic trend was unequivocal. When the data for 1970 become available, the probability is strong that they will confirm that this trend has continued. A move toward greater self-sufficiency was characteristic of all cities, from small to large, with the trend in large cities more pronounced.

A second critical finding relates to the continuing importance of exports between metropolitan centers. Over 11 million workers out of a total civilian labor force of 72 million were employed in the production of goods imported by metropolitan areas in 1960. Most of that trade is between cities; more than two-thirds of the 11 million workers were employed in one city producing goods and services imported by another city. Trade between metropolitan and non-metropolitan areas is declining both absolutely and even more relatively.

A third important finding of Knight's relates to the critical importance of the export sector because of its multiplier effect on local service employment. In the 1950s, 68 percent of the growth in metropolitan employment was related to the growth of the export sector; in the preceding decade the corresponding figure had been 84 percent. A significant ancillary finding is that much of the importance of the export sector derives from an increase in the value added by employees in that sector, not an increase in their numbers. Knight's most intriguing chapter is his case study of the rise and fall of

Huntsville, Alabama, in which he points out that while employment in that city grew by over 20,000 in the 1950s, net employment growth in the export sector was only 600. The key to the city's expansion was the shift in exports from low-productivity farming products to high-productivity space-related activities.

The fourth and last of Knight's important findings relates to the shifts in employment that follow the passing down of functions between large and smaller cities and between metropolitan and non-metropolitan areas. Low-productivity industries continue to leave large metropolitan centers that have relatively high wages, taxes, and rents. The magnitude of this shift is reflected in the loss by metropolitan areas of about 1 million export-sector jobs to non-metropolitan areas in 12 industrial categories with an average productivity of 29 percent below the national norm. In contrast, metropolitan areas made net gains in four industries—printing and publishing; other transportation equipment; finance, insurance, and real estate—(FIRE); and business and repair services—of 142,000 jobs. The few pages that Knight devotes to the economy of New York City—capital of the nation's business (in Chapter 5)—help to concretize these dynamic processes that have kept New York in the forefront of the nation's economy while its population has remained stable.

In the concluding pages of his book, the author calls attention to selected manpower problems that can be more effectively analyzed and treated by utilizing his methodology and findings. Because the primary interest and concern of the Conservation of Human Resources Project in metropolitan studies derive from its concern with strengthening manpower analysis and policy, I will elaborate on this relationship. Although we cannot expect specific manpower guidance from Knight's work, it may be possible to identify various leads for manpower policy from both his substantive findings and his general methodology.

His clear-cut finding that metropolitan areas are becoming ever more self-sufficient helps to explain the difficulties that policy-makers face if they seek to reverse the flow of people from non-metropolitan areas to our cities. The vast majority of new jobs are opening up in metropolitan areas, and people in search of jobs and careers will relocate in these larger aggregations. And as long as they do, they will reinforce the other factors leading to metropolitan expansion.

Knight's associated finding that cities tend to upgrade their job structures, exchanging high-productivity employment for the less attractive jobs that they continue to lose to non-metropolitan areas, means that there is an additional magnet to draw people from areas with surplus labor force and low wage rates.

Another finding of Knight's helps to explain why the passing down of low-productivity functions and jobs to non-metropolitan areas—a process of considerable scale and scope—fails to generate much secondary employment. On the one hand, the textile and apparel plants that flee the city tend to relocate in isolated rural areas, one plant to each community. The relatively low wages that they pay and their largely self-sufficient operations result in a low employment multiplier. The workers who get jobs in a new plant earn considerably more cash income than previously, and some local consumer-service industries are stimulated. But the momentum from the plant's payroll is not sufficient to start and maintain a self-generating cycle of local employment expansion.

The policy and program planners concerned with structuring a broad national approach to economic development, including the use of excess labor in depressed areas, must pay attention to the constraints on non-metropolitan growth that Knight's analysis illuminates. His findings give support to potential efforts to combine a wide array of governmental and private inputs to stimulate "growth centers" in the hope and expectation that, if investment can pass a critical point, the multiplier will take over and the preconditions for autonomous expansion will be established.

Several other suggestions for manpower policy and planning are scattered throughout Knight's analysis. For instance, his analysis emphasizes that large cities are under compulsion to keep upgrading their labor force. They must be on the alert at all times to encourage the expansion of high-productivity employment while bowing to the inevitable loss of less productive jobs. For city officials to concentrate on slowing the outflow of low-productivity jobs is likely to be effort wasted. They will be unable to constrain the forces of competition, and in devoting time and energy to this losing game, they will pass up important opportunities for encouraging the growth of more desirable jobs, better suited to the urban environment.

Knight's confirmation of the critical role played in the recent past by the rapid expansion of medical and educational services in stimulating the growth of employment is one more reason to inquire carefully about the near and distant future of these major industries. If, as many believe, their rapid growth is now leveling off, one must ask which industries are likely to take their place as major contributors to employment growth.

Many manpower implications can be drawn from Knight's fascinating account of the rise and fall of Huntsville, Alabama. The key lesson is that the omnipotent federal government must give more consideration than heretofore to the locations at which it establishes and expands major programs. Unless it concerns itself with the impact of its programs on manpower demand and supply, it is likely to generate unnecessary disruptions in local, regional, and even national labor markets, during expansion and particularly during contraction.

While it would repay the student of manpower to read Knight's book carefully to discern the full range of relationships between the changing structure of metropolitan trade and its labor-market impacts, the critical interface lies elsewhere. The key challenge that Knight's study precipitates lies in the realm of policy. What adjustments at different levels of government in the shaping of manpower policy hold promise of more effective outcomes?

The first lesson for policy-makers is that ours is a continental economy with substantial differences among and within regions. This means that there are severe limits on the ability of the federal government to design and implement a *national* manpower policy. At best, the federal government can set broad guidelines and undertake responsibility for much or all of the financing. But the specific plans must be shaped and carried out by the responsible agents in the labor market where the present and potential workers will live. The additional task that falls to the federal government is to work toward the shaping of a national development and location policy in the hope of using its large resources to speed the realization of priority goals such as slowing the inflow of rural migrants into our large metropolitan centers in favor of encouraging them to settle in embryonic growth centers closer to their homes.

At each level of government—federal, state, and local—Knight's approach underscores the desirability of much closer ties between the agencies and officials concerned with economic development and the manpower planners. His analyses demonstrate the powerful forces that are continually altering the competitive position of regions, local economies, industries. Even very large governmental programs are likely to have only a marginal impact on counter-manding or deflecting these underlying market forces. However, the more the leadership understands about the strength and direction of these underlying economic trends, the more likely that it will be able to design more effective manpower programs.

Finally, improved manpower planning and programming requires a marked improvement in the data base and in staff trained to assess the available data and to draw policy directions from them. A decennial census supple-mented by a limited number of industrial and county surveys does not produce even the minimum information required to monitor the broad changes that are occurring in the economy. Even more deficient is the information available about metropolitan areas. Although information, especially general informa-tion, is expensive to gather and process, and although information that is not analyzed and used to improve decision-making is of little or no value, it is difficult to see how the many new avenues of inquiry that Knight has opened up and that have potential for improved urban decision-making can be realized unless and until more effort is directed to improving the data base. Knight has demonstrated the mutually constructive interaction among conceptualization, empirical analysis, and policy. We should respond by working to improve all three.

CONTENTS

	Page
ACKNOWLEDGMENTS	vi
FOREWORD, by Eli Ginzberg	vii
LIST OF TABLES AND CHART	xv

Chapter

1   THE NATIONAL URBAN SYSTEM   1

     Some Principles of Urban Structure and Change   2
        The Metropolis as an Economic Organization   2
        The Income Multipliers   3
        The Provision of Government Services   4
        Growth of the Market, Economies of Scale, and
           Import Substitution   5
        External Economies and the Spawning of New Firms   5
        Availability of Finance   6
        Other Factors   6
        Implications for Analysis   7
     A Changing National Urban System   8
     Plan of the Study   12
     Notes   13

2   THE VALUE ADDED APPROACH TO MEASURING
     METROPOLITAN TRADE   14

     Estimating Metropolitan Production   15
     Estimating Metropolitan Requirements by Industry   19
     Treatment of Investment   20
     The Localized Nature of Private Household Services   22
     Estimating Exports and Imports and Converting to
        Employment Equivalents   22
     A Brief Mathematical Summary   22
     Summary and Conclusions   24
     Notes   24

3   A CASE STUDY: HUNTSVILLE, ALABAMA   26

     Trade in Huntsville at Three Points in Time   27

Chapter		Page
	Decadal Changes in Trade	30
	Job-Increase-Job-Decrease Analysis	36
	Measuring Import Substitution	37
	Implications for Huntsville in the 1970s	38
	Notes	39
4	THE TRADE MULTIPLIER	40
	Variation in the Trade Multiplier	41
	The Changing Value of the Multiplier	44
	Summary	47
	Notes	47
5	CHANGING PATTERNS OF METROPOLITAN TRADE	48
	Metropolitan and Non-metropolitan Growth Trends	48
	Major Changes in Aggregate Metropolitan Trade	51
	Decline of Importance of Trade in Metropolitan Employment	51
	Declining Importance of Trade with Non-metropolitan Areas and Increasing Importance of Inter-metropolitan Trade	53
	Changes in the Employment Terms of Trade	53
	Changes in Industry Trade Patterns	55
	Metropolitan Trade by Size of Place	55
	Metropolitan Trade by Type of Place	59
	Aggregate Trade and Employment Expansion	61
	Summary	64
6	REGIONAL TRADE PATTERNS	66
	Relative Importance of Inter- and Intra-regional Trade	66
	Interregional Trade	67
	Intraregional Trade	72
	Analysis of Three Industries	74
	Regional Trade Multipliers	76
	Summary	77
7	SPATIAL DYNAMICS OF EMPLOYMENT EXPANSION	78
	Geographic Shift of Export Activity	78
	The Directions of Geographic Shift	79
	Shifts from Metropolitan to Non-metropolitan Areas	81
	Shifts Between Size-of-Place Categories	81
	Shifts Between Regions	82
	Intraregional Shifts	82

Chapter		Page
	Geographic Concentration of Trade	88
	New York—Capital of the Nation's Business	95
	Summary	97
	Notes	97
8	KEY FINDINGS AND IMPLICATIONS	98
	Key Findings	98
	Implications of the Study	101
	Manpower Implications	105
	Notes	108
ABOUT THE AUTHOR		109
OTHER CONSERVATION OF HUMAN RESOURCES STUDIES— COLUMBIA UNIVERSITY		110

LIST OF TABLES AND CHART

Table		Page
1.1	Changing U.S. Urban System	10
2.1	Value Added per Employee	16
3.1	Metropolitan Trade in Huntsville, Alabama	28
3.2	Imports and Exports in Metropolitan Labor Market, Huntsville, Alabama	32
3.3	Analysis of Job Creation and Job Destruction by Industry in Huntsville, Alabama	34
4.1	Metropolitan Trade Multiplier by Type and Size Category of Place	42
4.2	Average VAPE and Average Metropolitan Trade Multiplier by Type of Place, 1960	43
4.3	Test Results	45
5.1	Growth Rates in Metropolitan and Non-metropolitan Areas	49
5.2	Most and Least Metropolitan Areas Compared	50
5.3	Metropolitan Trade, 368 Metropolitan Areas Combined	52
5.4	Metropolitan Trade by Type of Market	52
5.5	Metropolitan Exports and Imports by Industry	56
5.6	Metropolitan Trade by Size of Place	58
5.7	Industrial Composition of Employment in Exports by Type of Place, 1960	60
5.8	Aggregate Job-Increase-Job-Decrease Analysis	61
5.9	Analysis of Job Increases, 1950-60	63
6.1	Regional Trade Patterns by Industry, 1960	68
6.2	Regional Origin of Interregional Trade by Industry	70

Table   Page

6.3   Intraregional Trade   73

6.4   Inter- and Intra-regional Dimensions of Trade in Three
       Selected Industries, 1960   75

7.1   Geographic Shift of Export Activity   80

7.2   Measures of Metropolitan Shift of Exports, 1950-60   83

7.3   Changes in Interregional Export Trade, 1950-60   84

7.4   Intraregional Shift in Metropolitan Trade, 1950-60   86

7.5   Concentration Analysis   92

7.6   New York City's Share of Total Metropolitan Trade in
       Selected Industries   96

Chart

7.1   Geographic Concentration of Metropolitan Exports   89

Employment Expansion and Metropolitan Trade

CHAPTER

1

THE NATIONAL
URBAN SYSTEM

Transformation of the United States from an agrarian to an industrialized economy has reoriented and concentrated economic activity and growth around metropolitan-type areas. While metropolitan growth continues unabated, in recent decades the nature of the growth process has changed considerably; the role of manufacturing in the process of job creation is declining, and the role of services is in the ascendant. Emerging from this transitional phase of industrialization is a "new metropolism" that has important implications for growth, trade, and manpower.

What we are witnessing today is the reemergence of services as the major source of metropolitan growth after a century in which manufacturing was dominant. Early American cities served as centers of commerce and trade for their surrounding hinterlands, as exporters of raw materials, and as distribution points for imports. Located at strategic points along trade routes, the cities' growth depended on the growth of world markets for the raw materials they exported and the development of the producing hinterland. It was only during the last half of the nineteenth century that production replaced the exchange of goods as the basis of urban growth and new industrial cities achieved national prominence. Manufacturing activity was initially power- and resource-bound; workers migrated to take jobs in the growth industries. At that time, in contrast to the past 30 years, the primary criterion for growth was a favorable location or proximity to sources of energy and availability of raw materials required by the expanding industries.

A number of complex developments underlie the new metropolism, of which two are of central importance to the study at hand. First, consumers are allocating a larger share of income to the purchase of services produced within the local economy; moreover, productivity in the goods (primary and manufacturing) sector has been greater, and hence employment gains have been smaller, than in the service sector, which is largely tied to the city. Secondly, most expanding industries are becoming increasingly footloose and market-

1

oriented. These activities are expanding within or moving toward the larger metropolitan areas, while at the same time older export activities with low value added per employee (VAPE) have tended to move away. The result has been that metropolitan areas have become larger and more self-sufficient. This, in turn, has brought about changes in the magnitude and patterns of trade between metropolitan and non-metropolitan places and among regions within the American economy.

It is a central thesis of this study that an understanding of changes in metropolitan trade is fundamental to an understanding of urban growth and development. Yet no attempt has thus far been made to estimate the volume of trade among cities and between cities and non-metropolitan areas. The estimation of such trade is a major task of this study. Accordingly, an approach to measurement of trade among metropolitan economies and between these economies and non-metropolitan areas has been devised and applied for three census years, 1940, 1950, and 1960. Exports and imports are measured in terms of industrial classifications of employment and summarized for size-of-place and type-of-place categories as well as by regions and for the nation as a whole.*

The principal questions to which the book is addressed are (1) What is the nature of trade *within* the American economy? More specifically, to what extent do cities trade with each other and with non-metropolitan areas? In what industries is trade most important? (2) How have trade patterns changed over the last 20 years, and what are the implications of these trends? (3) What is the role of trade in the urban growth process? Do cities grow because they increase their traditional exports, develop new export activities, and/or replace imports with local production? (4) How useful is the concept of the trade multiplier as a tool for urban planning—that is, how stable is the relationship between total employment and employment in the export sector of a metropolitan economy?

SOME PRINCIPLES OF URBAN STRUCTURE AND CHANGE[1]

Preliminary to the analysis a brief statement is required relating to the structure of the metropolitan economy and the essential processes by which growth and development take place. It is within this framework that our study of metropolitan trade must be carried out.

The Metropolis as an Economic Organization

Fundamental to any discussion of the metropolitan economy is the observation that the metropolis is itself an economic organization. As in the

---

*Throughout this study, the terms "export" and "import" relate to the metropolitan economy. The city and its suburban area are regarded as an economy exporting and importing goods and to a lesser extent services as they trade with other metropolitan areas and non-metropolitan areas.

case of a nation or region, the metropolis exports certain goods and services and imports certain others in turn. Moreover, its economic organization is to a significant extent engaged in provision of goods and services to meet the needs of its own residents. Each industrial activity in a metropolis may be thought of as having its own market, which may be local, regional, national, or even international in scope. On a map these markets would be seen to overlap one another as well as the markets of industrial activities in other places.

Since there is great diversity in the economic structure of metropolitan areas, it is helpful to classify them in terms of two basic prototypes: nodal and non-nodal. The nodal metropolis is identifiable by a relatively high proportion of export activity in services, not in one or two consumer, business, or government services but rather in a group of services. This type of place generally serves as the metropolitan hub of its hinterland, an outlying area that the metropolis "structures" by providing it with services.

The non-nodal city is identified by a relatively high proportion of export activity in a restricted number of industry classifications. Although this type of place is perhaps most easily visualized as a city with relatively heavy concentrations of export activity in manufacturing, the classification would also include places with high concentrations of export activity in a particular services category such as hotels and entertainment, medical and educational, or government. The non-nodal place is simply a place in which there is a concentration of resources, usually in a more restricted number of economic activities in which it has some locational advantages. The non-nodal place has as its prime economic function the export of the limited line of goods or services in which it specializes to a regional or national market rather than the servicing of the needs of a hinterland.*

Two additional observations must be made regarding classification of metropolitan economies. The first is that many places will have mixed nodal/non-nodal characteristics and that classifications may change over time as functions are added or dropped by a metropolis. The second observation is that structural characteristics may be expected to vary with size of place. This would tend to be true because of opportunities for development of specialization arising out of economies of scale associated with larger local or export markets, because of the development of external economies, or because of diseconomies of scale.

The Income Multipliers

There are many sources of growth and many different growth processes that occur in metropolitan areas. Perhaps the most widely considered is the location of a new industry. It is common knowledge that the number of jobs created will be in excess of the additional workers employed by the industry itself. When employment increases as a result of the location of a new industry

---

*A hinterland may embrace a relatively small outlying area, in the case of small nodal places, or a very big region (even a section) in the case of larger nodal places.[2]

in a given city, there is a secondary or derived demand for labor that results from the respending of incomes within the city's boundaries. Persons receiving income from the firm in the form of wages, salaries, rents, interest, or profits spend a high proportion in the local consumer goods and services market, thereby generating additional demand for labor. Moreover, persons receiving this second "round" of income also spend a large part locally, generating still further income from which there are still additional "rounds" of spending.

It is very important to note, however, that not all of the income that is spent locally gives rise to new income within the community. The reason is, simply, that not all of the sales dollars remain within the local economy. Part of the expenditure is used to import goods and services from outside the city. In short, a part of the local consumer expenditure leaks out of the local economic system to pay for import components. The part that remains, however, comprises a demand for local resources, including labor.

The amplification process that results from local respending is generally designated by the term "income multiplier." The income multiplier is translated into an employment multiplier in Chapter 4. Needless to say, the size of the employment multiplier would vary with the type of new export firm that located within the metropolitan economy (that is, its tendency to generate local income in the form of wages and its wage level) as well as with type and size of place (that is, the propensity to spend income locally and the number of new jobs created per dollar of local spending for consumer goods and service will vary with local availability of goods and services and size of business infrastructure).

The Provision of Government Services

As usually formulated in aggregative economic analysis, the income multiplier treats only the respending for consumer goods and services. Government spending is regarded as an autonomous injection of income into the stream, one that will have its own multiplier effect. Local government services include, however, a variety of activities closely associated with consumer and business needs, such as police and fire protection, provision of recreational services, and operation of schools. Changes in the level of such activities are probably not closely tied to the level of local income in the short run, but over a more extended period they are likely to be rather closely associated. If such observations are correct, we may conclude that when employment increases as a result of the location of a new (export) firm in a given city, there tends to be a secondary or derived demand for labor due to an increase in government services. This secondary effect is analogous to the multiplier effect due to local respending of income. Thus, in addition to the jobs generated in retailing and consumer services, there would be jobs generated in the public school system, in the parks system, and in city hall. In short, there are jobs generated for services in the local public sector as well as in the local private sector.

4

Growth of the Market, Economies of Scale, and Import Substitution

Another important concept in the economics of urban growth is that there are minimum efficient sizes for various types of firms. This means that the market must be of a certain size before the establishment of a firm can be justified. The size of the market required to make a firm economically viable is called the "critical size" of the market. As a metropolis grows, and the local market becomes larger, these critical sizes are reached for more and more activities; as a result, local or nonresident investors enter the market and set up shop.

The result of establishing such new firms is, of course, to increase the output destined for use within the metropolis, thereby resulting in import substitution. If the newly formed firm produces parts, supplies, or business services previously purchased outside the city's economy, there will be *import substitution that serves to increase local employment engaged in supplying inputs to local business.* If the newly formed firm provides consumer services or goods previously purchased outside the city's economy, there will again be *import substitution that serves to increase employment but this time in the consumer goods and services sector.* In both cases employment expansion arising from import substitution will be amplified by the income multiplier effect.

To sum up, as growth occurs in the city, a series of critical market-size thresholds are passed, which cause successive enlargements of local employment by increasing the consumer's propensity to consume locally and by increasing the volume of inputs purchased in the local market by the firms supplying the needs of local consumers or exporting goods and services to outside markets. Such import substitution has the effect of amplifying the initial employment expansion that set it off.

External Economies and the Spawning of New Firms

A closely related concept is that of external economies of scale. This term has come to apply to economies that are "external" to a firm but result from the demand created by the prior establishment of other user firms. Firms that supply these external economies provide services or goods that the user firm would otherwise have to provide for itself. Examples of external economies are found in most of the business services (for example, advertising agencies, accountants, data-processing service bureaus) and in a number of manufacturing firms that produce on contract (for example, producers of parts, job printers).*

---

*The externalizing of a service will be picked up in the data as a job shift from the externalizing industry to the external industry—e.g., from banking to mainly business services. There will not be an increase in jobs, however. To the contrary, since economies have taken place, it is not unlikely that there will be a decrease in numbers of persons employed.

We refer here to economies that come about when the user firm contracts out rather than produces the good or service within its own organization (in-house). In the previous section we referred simply to substitution of goods or services locally produced for those goods or services that were previously imported. In either case the supplying firm exists because thresholds of critical market size have been overcome.

In the latter case the impetus to grow lies in the fact that the existence of the supplying firm is an attraction to firms to locate within the city. Since firms may secure basic business services and even certain component parts and materials outside of their own organization, they may operate with a smaller investment of capital and with a less elaborate organization. Such conditions permit a city to compete with other cities for new firms and also to encourage would-be local entrepreneurs to organize new business.

Availability of Finance

Still another possible route by which growth in a city's economy may feed upon itself is through the increased availability of finance. In practice there are barriers to the ready flow of risk capital from one area to another, especially where small and medium-sized firms are concerned. All other things being the same, a successful businessman in Houston would prefer to invest in a new enterprise in the Houston area rather than one in some small township located a great distance away. As regards short-term credit, banks prefer to lend to local firms whose operations can be fairly accurately and continuously evaluated rather than to distant enterprises, with whom communication is more difficult.

Moreover, the existence of an atmosphere in which general growth is occurring and in which profits tend to rise from one year to the next serves to bring about a greater willingness on the part of individuals and firms to invest in new enterprises.

Perhaps of even greater importance is the increased *ability* of local banks to extend loans. When new firms enter the market and begin to make payments to employees and local suppliers, demand deposits will increase in local banks and the reserve position of these banks will be improved. The result, of course, is an increased supply of short-term credit in the metropolitan economy.

The consequence of these combined tendencies is that once growth begins to occur in a city, availability of new financing may improve sharply, providing an important stimulus to still further growth.

Other Factors

The preceding sections do not exhaust the factors that cause growth to become cumulative. As the metropolitan economy grows, its labor market broadens and tends to become more heterogeneous. Increasingly, firms find

6

that they can readily procure the special skills they require. This ready availability of labor, along with availability of external economies and finance mentioned above, make the metropolis an attractive place to locate.

Moreover, the need to be close to customers, to sources of finance, and to competitors increasingly provides a locational pull as the area grows. As more firms locate for these and other reasons examined above, the centripetal force becomes even greater.

An additional point is that the growth of the metropolitan economy and its ability to service the needs of the hinterland may cause firms to locate within the hinterland even if space or other factors rule out locating within the metropolis itself. Such location of firms increases the size of the metropolis's external market and results in still further tendencies toward economies of scale, external economies, and the spawning of new firms.

Needless to say, there are negative aspects to the growth process. The increasing size of the metropolis brings increasing rental costs, overhead costs, and costs of congestion and administration to the public sector. For a number of reasons, wages tend to be higher in metropolitan areas. Thus firms face increasing problems, relating to the cost and availability of usable space and to the cost of a number of other inputs. These factors cause some firms to leave at the same time that others are entering. Increasingly, as the metropolis grows, the constraints on further growth become more numerous and severe, and only the viable firms can survive.

The constraints are, however, likely to lead to an upgrading of the export sector and to the increasing self-sufficiency of the metropolis. As the more viable firms bid away the metropolitan resources, the less viable firms are forced to move to other lower-cost areas, where they may remain competitive in the industry. In short, the export sector is upgraded as the viable firms expand and the least viable leave. Moreover, as a result of the upgrading process, income and investment funds generated by the export sector will increase, thus causing an increase in the secondary demand for local goods and services. Consequently, even though the number of export jobs may not increase and may even decline, the upgrading process should eventually lead to an expansion and broadening (through import substitution) of the local sector with a concomitant increase in the income multiplier. It is even likely that resources will be bid away from the less viable export firms by firms being established (import substitution) or expanded in the local sector.

Implications for Analysis

In general, this discussion indicates that cities alter their function and structure as they grow. Significant differences in structure among the size-of-place categories appear as a logical process of growth, with larger places reflecting the effects of external economies and economies of scale in the composition of their labor forces.

A second and closely related implication relates to patterns of trade. From what has been said, it is clear that employment expansion may be expected to

7

be concentrated in different industrial classifications at different stages of growth of a metropolis. As the metropolitan economy grows larger, the development of external economies and the increase in market size should be evident by the increasingly important role of the local sector in the employment growth process. This trend is further accentuated by trends toward faster rates of productivity increases and slower rates of employment growth in manufacturing (export-type) industries than in service categories, which tend to dominate the local sector (although certain of them are exported to a significant degree). These trends lead to a relative increase in the importance of the local sector in employment terms.[3]

Growth in small metropolitan economies will be more dependent on growth of export activity than will growth in large metropolises. For one thing, small places have a less developed local sector and a smaller income multiplier. Second, export activity will represent a considerably larger share of total employment, thus making the small metropolis more vulnerable to employment growth trends in its export sector.

It should be noted that as metropolitan areas grow and as their local sectors expand, metropolitan trade will decline in those activities most subject to import substitution. Import substitution implies the loss of export markets for those areas that have traditionally been exporting such goods or services. Further, as the entire system of cities expands in terms of population and income market, size increases sufficiently that cities lower on the hierarchy are able to take over new and more sophisticated export roles (for example, Atlanta and Dallas firms take over sophisticated financial, legal, and merchandising functions within their regions that were previously performed in New York).

In both instances there is a shift in the performance of activities that previously provided an export for some metropolitan economy. Economies so affected must compensate for the loss of such jobs by increased exports to areas not yet subject to import substitution, by increased exports in export activities evolving from new technology and the demand for new goods and services, or by the expansion of their local sectors as outlined above.

A CHANGING NATIONAL URBAN SYSTEM

In understanding the network of trade relationships, one must view the national economy as composed of a system of metropolitan areas. This system of urban places may best be conceptualized as a hierarchy, with villages and towns at the base and national and international metropolises at the apex.[4] The hierarchical structuring of metropolitan areas may be attributed, in part, to factors affecting the location of economic activity—in particular, the level at which a particular activity is performed.

The higher up the hierarchy an activity is performed, the more geographically concentrated the activity. National administrative functions, whether for the public, private, or nonprofit sector, tend to be concentrated in national centers; regional functions tend to be somewhat more dispersed. Where plant

8

economies of scale obtain or where plants are resource-bound, industries tend to be geographically concentrated. Moreover, some activities tend to cluster for other reasons. External economies are often realized in a local agglomeration of activities in the form of industrial or service complexes, such as industrial or office parks, resort towns, research and development centers, and central business districts.

The position of a city in the national urban system or hierarchy may thus be approximated by the level to which its export activities are directed. The highest-order activities are generally considered to be those that compete in international markets. Locations where these activities are concentrated are generally designated as international metropolises (for example, the money markets in New York, London, and Paris). In descending order follow national regional, and various subregional centers—state capitals, county seats, villages, and hamlets. It should be apparent that as one ascends the hierarchy, the number of activities performed tends to increase; lower-order functions plus additional ones are carried out. In turn the number of places where higher-order activities are carried on decreases.

It is within the hierarchy or system of urban places that an urban area grows. But the hierarchy itself is continuously being modified as changes occur in the national parameters. Changes in technology, especially in communications and transportation, tend to alter the level at which an activity is carried on. Changes in taste, in income distribution, in the income elasticities of demand, will affect the mix of goods and services that are in demand. Changes in technology of production and in the size of markets will affect the mix of factors—land, labor, and capital—required and in turn will affect the decision as to where an industry should locate or expand.

In the United States, economic growth has taken new forms that are reflected in the continual spatial restructuring of the economy. While the national urban system emerged, according to Eric Lampard and Beverly Duncan, during the last half of the nineteenth century,[5] major changes have occurred since then in the ordering of metropolitan areas by population size. (See Table 1.1.) The midwestern metropolises St. Louis and Chicago surpassed the East Coast cities Boston and Baltimore during the 1860s, and by 1880 San Francisco, the first major West Coast port, and Pittsburgh, the "first great heavy industrial agglomeration," ranked among the largest 10 places. The rise to prominence of Cleveland, Buffalo, and Minneapolis-St. Paul during the 1880s and of Detroit and Milwaukee during the 1890s represented the growth of resource-oriented manufacturing industries in the Great Lakes region. More recent entrants include Los Angeles and Kansas City during the early 1900s, Indianapolis during the 1920s, Houston in the 1940s, Dallas, San Diego, San Antonio, and Miami in the 1950s, and Memphis in the 1960s.

Cities that have not grown or have lost their competitive edge have descended in the hierarchy. Very often, such cities are located in declining areas, are old, have few or no new or expanding industries, are dependent on declining industries, have outdated social infrastructures, or are not attractive to other industries. Charleston, S.C., for example, has declined from the fourth largest city in 1790 to 170th largest in 1960. Pittsburgh declined from 10th largest city in 1940 to 22d largest in 1970. Small nodal metropolitan areas that

9

TABLE 1.1

Changing U.S. Urban System
(cities ranked by population, 1790-1970)*

Cities	All Over 5,000 1790	All Over 5,000 1800	1850	1900	1910	1920	1930	1940	1950	1960	1970 (prelim-inary)
Albany, N.Y.	*		8	39	50	60	64	65	68	93	125
Atlanta, Ga.			*	42	31	33	32	28	33	24	27
Baltimore, Md.	5	3	3	6	7	8	8	7	6	6	7
Boston, Mass.	3	4	4	5	5	7	9	9	10	13	16
Buffalo, N.Y.			12	8	10	11	13	14	15	20	28
Charleston, S.C.	4	5	11	67	90	103	148	129	170	*	*
Chicago, Ill.			19	2	2	2	2	2	2	2	2
Cincinnati, Ohio		*	6	10	13	16	17	17	18	21	29
Cleveland, Ohio			32	7	6	5	6	6	7	8	10
Columbus, Ohio			29	27	29	28	28	26	28	28	21
Dallas, Tex.			n.a.	87	58	42	33	31	22	14	8
Denver, Col.			n.a.	25	27	25	29	24	24	23	25
Detroit, Mich.			23	13	9	4	4	4	5	5	5
Houston, Tex.			*	84	68	45	26	21	14	7	6
Indianapolis, Ind.			53	21	22	21	21	20	23	26	11
Jacksonville, Fla.			n.a.	99	93	78	59	51	50	61	23
Jersey City, N.J.			56	17	19	22	23	30 (301,173)	37	47	53
Kansas City, Mo.			n.a.	22	20	19	19	19	20	27	26
Los Angeles, Cal.			*	35	17	10	5	5	4 (369,129)	3	3
Louisville, Ky.	*		10	18	24	29	24	25	30	31	38
Lowell, Mass.	*		18	38	46	61	93	88	111	*	*
Memphis, Tenn.			51	36	37	40	36	32	26	22	17
Milwaukee, Wisc.			28	14	12	13	12	13	13	11	12
Minneapolis, Minn.				19	18	18	16	16	17	25	31
Mobile, Ala.			25	92	107	116	129	118	77	62	67
Newark, N.J.	*		15	'16 (108,027)	14	15	18	18	21	(405,220) 30	35
New Haven, Conn.	*		26	30	35	39	49	54	59	81	101
New Orleans, La.			5	12	15	17	15	15	16	15	19
Newport, R.I.	7		n.a.	*	*	*	*	*	*	*	*

10

City										
New York, N.Y.	2	2	1	1	1	1	1	1	1	1
Oakland, Cal.			n.a.	55	32	31	30 (284,063)	29	27	33	37
Philadelphia, Pa.	1	1	2	3	3	3	3	3	3	4	4
Phoenix, Ariz.			*	*	*	*	*	149	98	29	20
Pittsburgh, Pa.		*	9	11	8	9	10	10	12	16	24
Portland, Me.		*	24	77	91	101	125	128	148	*	*
Portland, Ore.			n.a.	41	28	24	25	27	29	32	34
Portsmouth, N.H.	*	9	(6,380)	*	*	*	*	*	*	*	*
Providence, R.I.	8	7	13	20	23	27	37	37	43	56	70
Richmond, Va.	*	8	21	45	39	38	44	45	46	52	56
Rochester, N.Y.	*		16	24	25	23	22	23	32	38	48
St. Louis, Mo.	*		7	4	4	6 (234,698)	7	8	8	10	18
St. Paul, Minn.		*	*	23	26	30	31	33	35	40	45
Salem, Mass.	6	6	27	*	*	*	*	*	*	*	*
San Antonio, Tex.			*	70	54	41	38	36	25	17	15
San Diego, Cal.			*	*	*	93	53	43	31	18	14
San Francisco, Cal.			17	9	11	12	11	12	11	12	13
San Jose, Cal.		(5,166) 11	*	*	*	*	152	145	118	57	(445,779) 30
Savannah, Ga.	*		35	68	86	85	102	99	87	82	121
Seattle, Wash.			n.a.	47	21	20	22	22	19	19	22
Syracuse, N.Y.			22	29	34 (168,497)	37	40	41	47	53	65
Toledo, Ohio		*	*	26	30	26	27	34	36	39	33
Troy, N.Y.	*		20 (17,565)	61	72	98	122	131	160	*	*
Utica, N.Y.			30	65	73	74	89	92	106	129	*
Washington, D.C.	*		14	15	16	14	14	11	9	9	9
Worcester, Mass.	*		33	28	33	35	42	44	50	66	72

Note: Population size of city ranking thirtieth written above "30" for each year; n.a.: not available.

*The 30 highest-ranking (in population) cities are listed for each year. The ranks of these cities are also indicated in other census years unless the city's population was less than 5,000 people before 1900; less than 50,000 between 1900 and 1950; or less than 100,000 in 1960 or 1970, in which case an asterisk appears.

Sources: A Century of Population Growth: From the First Census of the U.S. to the 12th, 1790-1900, U.S. Department of Commerce, Bureau of the Census (Washington, D.C.), pp. 11-78; *Statistical View of the U.S.: Compendium of the 7th Census* (Washington, D.C., 1854), p. 192; *Statistical Abstract of the U.S.: 1912, 1957, 1969* (Washington, D.C.); *1970 Census of Population,* PC(1)-A1, Table 28 (Washington, D.C., 1971).

service agricultural hinterlands declined with the decreasing demand for these services.

The emergence of major megalopolises may require a new conceptual framework. Urban growth has tended in recent times to be concentrated in a few clusters of metropolitan areas.[6] Names have already been assigned to four such clusters: Bos-Wash to the area between Boston and Washington; San-San to the areas between San Francisco and San Diego; Chic-Pitt to the area between Chicago and Pittsburgh; and Mijacks to the area between Miami and Jacksonville.[7] The major consequence of a continuation of such clustered growth will be that densities, with all commensurate benefits and problems, will increase. It will not be possible to keep densities down by territorial expansion, for there is very little space left to be filled within these clusters.

In contrast, there are lagging or depressed areas that lie at the interstices of regional systems. Efforts to deal with the problems of these areas such as the Appalachian regional development plan have not met with much success. If these areas are viewed as part of the national urban system rather than as regions unto themselves, more effective development policies could be structured.[8]

This study is based on the assumption that analyses of economic growth and employment expansion should be cast in a framework that specifically recognizes the spatial dimension and, further, that the spatial restructuring of the national economy is an important ongoing process that must be dealt with explicitly. The effectiveness of policies for national, regional, and urban growth will depend in no small part on how well we understand spatial organization and the spatial dynamics of growth.

PLAN OF THE STUDY

This introduction is the first of eight chapters that together comprise the entire study. The second chapter explains the nature and merits of a new method—the value added approach—for measuring metropolitan trade. This method is then applied to one urban area, Huntsville, Alabama (See Chapter 3), to demonstrate the new insights it is capable of providing in the analysis of metropolitan growth.

In Chapter 4 the relationships between employment in export-oriented activity (the export sector) and total metropolitan employment (that is, the trade multiplier) is examined and the actual relationship is established. The discussion then focuses on whether the relationship is stable or whether it will change as the community grows and as the national parameters change.

Chapter 5 analyzes changes in patterns of trade and in the importance of trade between metropolitan and non-metropolitan areas and among metropolitan places. Changes in terms of trade are noted both between metropolitan and non-metropolitan places and for different sizes and types of place.

In Chapter 6 regional trade patterns are examined. Trends in importance of interregional and intraregional trade are noted. Chapter 7 presents a somewhat different analysis of economic changes in which spatial shifts in trade are measured among metropolitan areas and non-metropolitan areas, among and within regions, and among sizes of place. Finally, in Chapter 8 the major findings are summarized and the implications of the findings for manpower policy are pointed out.

NOTES

1. This section is drawn largely from Thomas M. Stanback and Richard V. Knight, *The Metropolitan Economy: The Process of Employment Expansion* (New York: Columbia University Press, 1970), pp. 56-73.

2. *Ibid.*, pp. 49-50.

3. National trends in productivity in the goods and services sectors are analyzed by Victor Fuchs, *Growing Importance of the Service Industries* (New York: National Bureau of Economic Research, 1965).

4. For a discussion of the urban system, see Eric F. Lampard, "The Evolving System of Cities: Urbanization and Economic Development," in Harry S. Perloff and Lowdon Wingo, Jr., eds., *Issues in Urban Economics* (Baltimore: The Johns Hopkins Press, 1968).

5. *Ibid.*, p. 89.

6. The term "megalopolis" has been applied to the urbanized region lying between Boston and Washington, D.C., by Jean Gottman, in *Megalopolis* (New York: Twentieth Century Fund, 1961).

7. Jack Rosenthal, "Stans Warns of 'Anthill Society'," The *New York Times* 119 (October 9, 1969), p. 28.

8. See Niles Hansen, *Rural Poverty and the Urban Crisis* (Bloomington: Indiana University Press, 1970), chapter 6.

2

THE VALUE ADDED APPROACH
TO MEASURING METROPOLITAN
TRADE

The task of the present chapter is to explain the procedure used to measure trade within the U.S. economy. Estimates obtained serve as a basis for studying trade links among metropolitan areas and for determining the impact that changes in trade activity have on employment expansion in metropolitan areas.

Since no measures of metropolitan exports and imports are available from government sources, trade flows must be estimated indirectly.[1] The basic approach that will be used for estimating trade in 31 industries in each of 368 metropolitan places is simple and consists of three major steps:* (1) estimation of production, in value added terms, in each metropolitan place; (2) estimation of requirements of the metropolis; and (3) determination of the amount of exports or imports in the metropolis by subtraction of requirements from production.

Previous techniques for estimating metropolitan trade have relied on employment data alone and are limited to export activity. In most instances requirements have been seen in terms of the average allocation of employment among industries for the nation as a whole. Each metropolitan economy has been regarded as having a balance of trade in terms of employment, with exports and imports measured as positive or negative differences from this national pattern of employment composition.[3] Such procedures do not permit analysis of the changing characteristics of metropolitan trade in terms of the

---

*Of the 368 metropolitan labor markets included in this study 214 are standard metropolitan statistical areas (SMSAs); the remaining metropolitan units are counties that contain cities of more than 25,000 population (1960) but that are not part of an SMSA as usually defined.[2] It should be noted that the U.S. Bureau of the Budget annually reviews the definitions of each metropolitan area and revises when necessary. In order to ensure comparability in making intertemporal comparisons the same (1965) definitions are used for all three census years in this study.

upgrading of the value of production and the altering of the metropolitan terms of trade within the national economy. It is to deal with these very aspects of growth that the value added approach used here has been devised.

ESTIMATING METROPOLITAN PRODUCTION

As noted above, in past studies (generally known as export-base studies) employment has nearly always been used as the estimator of production. While census employment data are the most reliable and detailed industry statistics available at the community (county) level and are used here in estimating production, they are not an accurate measure of production when used alone. Employment data indicate only the number of employees in a local industry, not the income generated locally in the process of production. Yet it is the income generated locally that determines the metropolitan income, that is, the level of community expenditures for consumption and investment of goods and services, and thus the community's total requirements of goods and services. It is for this reason that employment data need adjustment to reflect the full value of production.

Income generated in the process of production is generally referred to as the value added by an industry—sales less all costs of intermediate goods and services incurred in the production process. Included in value added are all payments to the factors of production—land, labor, and capital. More specifically, value added includes wages, interest, rent, depreciation of plant and equipment, and profits.

It is these value added estimates that are used to impute value and income generated to the employment data for each industry category in each metropolitan place in the economy. The procedure involves two steps. In the first, value added by production in an industrial category in the U.S. economy in a given year (that is, the industry's contribution to national income) is divided by the average number of employees in that industry to secure the value-estimating statistic—value added per employee (VAPE).[4] The VAPE statistic for each industry category is presented in Table 2.1. In the second, the VAPE for the industry is multiplied by the number of employees in that industry in a given metropolitan area to estimate that area's total value of production in the industry.

The VAPE varies considerably among industries, since it depends on the proportions in which the factors are utilized and on the rate of renumeration applicable to each factor as well as on the level of profits. In fact, factor proportions vary widely among industries. Of 321 detailed industry classifications studied by the Area Development Administration of the U.S. Department of Commerce in 1957, investment per employee exceeded $15,000 in 32 and was below $1,500 in 38 others.[5] Further, whereas the cost of labor accounted for over 40 percent of total costs in 27 industries, it accounted for less than 10 percent in 26 others.[6]

The index of VAPE per annum used below should be regarded as an index of income generated, not as an index of industry productivity. There are many

15

TABLE 2.1

Value Added per Employee

Industry	Dollars			Percent of National Average		
	1940	1950	1960	1940	1950	1960
Primary						
Agriculture	762	2,602	3,582	46	64	57
Forestry, fisheries	821	2,592	3,455	49	64	55
Mining	2,002	5,439	7,777	120	133	124
Construction	1,334	3,501	5,787	80	86	92
Manufacturing						
Food, kindred products	1,971	4,220	6,717	118	103	107
Textile mills	1,236	3,493	4,831	74	86	77
Apparel manufacturing	1,231	2,851	3,943	74	70	63
Lumber manufacturing	1,261	3,371	4,774	75	83	76
Printing, publishing	2,157	4,524	6,784	129	111	108
Chemicals, allied	3,154	7,713	10,982	189	189	174
Electrical, other machinery	2,644	5,085	7,503	158	125	119
Motor vehicles, equipment	2,939	8,207	11,883	176	201	189
Other transportation, equipment	2,702	4,629	7,650	161	114	121
Other miscellaneous manufacturing	2,192	5,420	8,106	131	133	129
Utilities	4,122	7,007	14,226	246	172	226
Mainly Business Services						
Railroad, railway express	2,534	5,151	8,065	151	126	128
Trucking, warehousing	1,747	4,015	6,549	104	98	104
Other transportation	2,316	4,928	9,853	138	121	112
Communications	2,560	4,602	9,853	153	113	156
Wholesale	2,233	5,108	7,484	133	125	119
FIRE	5,153	10,899	16,593	308	267	264
Business, repair services	1,584	3,429	5,441	95	84	86
Mainly Consumer Services						
Retailing*	1,472	3,379	4,481	88	83	71
Hotel, other personal services	1,062	2,420	3,485	63	59	55
Entertainment, recreation	1,800	3,121	4,654	108	77	74
Private households	555	1,504	2,379	33	37	38
Medical, other professions	1,798	3,330	5,062	107	82	80
Government						
Public administration	1,430	3,201	5,334	85	78	85
Armed forces	1,067	3,115	4,269	64	76	68
Total	1,673	4,078	6,297	100	100	100

*Combines three retailing classifications: food and dairy stores, eating and drinking places, and other retailing.

Source: National Income and Product Accounts of the U.S., 1929-1965, U.S. Department of Commerce, Office of Business Economics (Washington, D.C.: G.P.O., 1966). National Income by Industry, Table 1.12, pp. 18-21. Number of persons engaged in production, Table 6.6, pp. 110-113.

measures of productivity; each has been developed to answer particular questions, yet none provides a really satisfactory index of factor productivity.[7] It is important, therefore, not to view VAPE as an index of productivity that is attributable to labor alone, but rather to view it as an index of income generated in the process of production.

That industries differ significantly to the extent to which they generate income can be demonstrated by a comparison of VAPE indices calculated for national industries. If we consider the classifications used in this study, the industry with the lowest VAPE is private households and the industry with the highest is finance, insurance, and real estate (FIRE).* Their actual values in 1960 were $2,400 and $16,000, respectively, compared with the national average of $6,300. Thus, we see that the assumption that income generated per employee is the same in all industries, an assumption implicit in earlier metropolitan studies using employment data alone, is clearly not in accordance with fact. Needless to say, VAPE will tend to rise through time as a result of the increasing factor prices that have characterized the American economy during the postwar period. More important, however, it should be noted that the relative levels of industry VAPEs are likely to change over time. Such relative change would obtain with a change either in the proportions in which the factors are used or in the rate of remuneration to the factors. For example, the introduction of new production technology may require increased investment in plant and equipment without commensurate increase in employment or with a reduction in employment, resulting in a higher VAPE. The same development may result also in an upgrading of the skill mix of labor, thus increasing wage levels and increasing VAPE even further. An increase may also come about if labor productivity increases with no increase in other factor inputs (providing these productivity gains are at least partially reflected in higher wages), or if unions improve their bargaining positions and negotiate wage increases that are passed on to the customer. Moreover, the market structure may change, enabling producers to increase prices and profits.

The significance of the above becomes apparent when we consider employment in trade activity. In a community's export sector, the value added associated with each person employed in FIRE is almost five times that of a person engaged in agriculture or mining, four times that of a person in apparel, almost three times that of a person in public administration, and so on. Therefore, if the value of imports and exports are to be in balance in each community, a community would have to export the output associated with five agricultural or mining workers or four apparel workers, in exchange for importing the output associated with one person employed in FIRE. This relationship, which we shall call the "employment terms of trade" (ETOT; expressed as the ratio of the employment equivalent of imports to employment in export activity), may be quite low—well below 100 (1:1)—in a mining town or quite high—well above 100—in a regional center. If, as in most economic-base studies, no allowance is made for VAPE differences, the value of each

---

*There are very difficult problems that must be dealt with in imputing value added to the output of banks and insurance companies, and the solutions that have been improvised may result in overestimation for the FIRE category.

worker's output would be taken as the same, irrespective of industry category, and the employment terms of trade are assumed (implicitly) to be identical (100) in all communities. We shall return to a consideration of ETOT in Chapter 4.

The method used in estimating VAPE for each industry category within a metropolitan area does not, of course, take into consideration differences among metropolitan areas other than those relating to industrial composition. Personal-income differences in the export sector will affect the level of personal incomes throughout the community, frequently in a direct fashion by way of a wage "roll-out" effect from the industry or industries that dominate the community's economy to those in the local sector. Communities with above-average shares of employment in industries having high levels of value added (motor vehicles, for example) tend to have a higher than average factor costs, such as wages, throughout their economies. Similarly, a community's average wage levels will be low if there is concentration of industries with low value added, such as mining, apparel, food-processing, textiles, or armed forces. As a consequence, these places will not be able to support as broad a range of activities locally as do places with high VAPE exports.

Although the estimates may have failed to account fully for this effect, the range of measured average metropolitan VAPE attributable to variations in the industrial composition of the work force is considerable and attests to the usefulness of the weighting procedure. In 1960, average VAPE ranged from $4,832 in Fayetteville, North Carolina, or 23 percent below the national average of $6,297, to $8,416 in Flint, Michigan, or 34 percent above. Average productivity for all metropolitan areas combined was on average 21 percent higher than in non-metropolitan areas.

A second source of variation among metropolitan areas arises as a result of variations in value added within a given industry category. Value added may vary because technology varies among the industry subcategories that make up an industrial classification (for example, among the various types of spinning, weaving, and knitting establishments within the textile products category), and these various branches of an industry may be located in different places.

Moreover, average value added is not the same in all metropolitan economies. If economies of scale can be realized in an industry, productivity in the industry will increase with the size of the market. Insofar as size of place reflects the size of market and thus the economies of scale realized by industries in the local sector, productivity may be to some extent a function of the size of place. If we suppose, for example, that capital intensity or factor costs in "other retail stores" increase with size of place, value of output in this industry will be underestimated in large places and overestimated in small places. This in turn distorts to some extent the estimated patterns of metropolitan trade: Exports of retail services will be underestimated in large places and overestimated in small places. Moreover, the supply of factors, especially labor, will vary considerably by place.

18

ESTIMATING METROPOLITAN REQUIREMENTS BY INDUSTRY

After calculating production in VAPE terms the next step in estimating trade activity is to determine the community's requirements from each industry. Local requirements include all of the community's needs—private and public, consumption and investment—for the output of an industry. Since requirements are to be compared to production in each industry, both measures must be expressed in the same units and for the same industry categories. Requirements, therefore, cannot be expressed in terms of the usual categories of expenditures (classes of consumer or investment goods and services) but must instead be expressed in terms of their industrial composition. Moreover, requirements are expressed in terms of value added by the industry in question not in terms of the total value of its finished product.

The procedure devised to estimate requirements by industry involves two steps: first, total metropolitan requirements are estimated as being equal to total metropolitan factor income (that is, to total value added in production); secondly, requirements are allocated among industry categories.

There is reason to believe that the value added approach will estimate metropolitan income with acceptable accuracy. Others have shown that industry differences explain a large part of the variance in average per capita incomes by states. There would seem to be no reason to expect them to explain a lesser proportion of the variation in metropolitan incomes. Perloff found that about 75 percent of the variance in state incomes could be explained by productivity differences among national industries. The greatest variance between his estimates, based on the industrial composition of employment in each state, and the estimates of state income published by the U.S. Department of Commerce were in the low-income states of the Southeast.[8] A similar study by Hanna utilizing more detailed industry categories (140 compared to 58 in the Perloff study), resulted in much the same findings.[9] The unexplained variance was attributed largely to regional wage differentials.

It must be recognized that a community's income and hence its expenditures may differ from the value of its product to the extent that net factor payments or transfer payments are made to nonresidents. Participation income—wages, salaries, and income from unincorporated enterprises— is paid almost entirely to local residents, but property income—corporate profits, interest, and rental income to persons—may go to nonresidents. An outflow of factor payments to nonresidents will be offset, however, to the extent that local residents receive income from property outside their community or from transfer payments. In the value added approach it is assumed that there is no net flow of income payments (including transfers) either into or out of a community and, therefore, that metropolitan income is equal to the value added by production, or the metropolitan product.

In allocating total requirements of a metropolis among industries, the basic assumption is that the industrial composition of these requirements (that is, the requirements mix) is the same as for the nation as a whole. For example, in 1960, 2.07 percent of metropolitan income was allocated to requirements produced by the motor vehicle industry in every community.

Although the requirements-mix assumption implies that the same goods and services are required in the same proportions in every community, it is recognized that life-style varies from place to place. This cannot, of course, be taken into account in the estimating procedure. What is assumed is simply that factors such as climate, size and type of place, and mean per capita incomes, which affect a community's life-style, are not great enough to affect significantly the accuracy of estimates of the industrial composition of the community's total requirements for goods and services.

Unfortunately, it is not possible to test this important assumption. Where local requirements have been studied, as in consumer expenditure surveys, they have been classified according to the type of final product, such as housing, automobiles and transportation, medical and personal care—classifications that are difficult to break down into industrial components. For the broad categories used in this study, the assumption is probably valid. Average demand per employee for the aggregate output of an industry should be similar in all metropolitan areas. If very detailed industrial classifications are used, such as men's winter clothing or ladies' swimwear, one would expect significant variations in local demand. It is even possible that the more detailed the industry classifications, the less reliable will be the estimates.

It is implicit in the requirements-mix assumption that the community's requirements in an industry represent the aggregate of all the different sectors of a community. Insofar as there are variations among communities in the industrial composition of requirements of a given sector (public sector, private sector) or in the distribution of local requirements among sectors, there will be variations in the industrial composition of total local requirements. For purposes of this study, however, it is assumed that industrial composition of each sector's requirements, as well as each sector's proportion of total local requirements, is the same in every community.

TREATMENT OF INVESTMENT

The treatment of investment deserves special discussion. No allowance is made for the shift in investment funds. Production of investment goods and services is recorded in value added terms in the communities in which production takes place and shows up largely as net exports from these places. Investment requirements are estimated at the place where they are ultimately consumed. They are implicit in the estimates of total requirements computed for each community. Investment goods and services are considered to be traded in the same way as other types of goods and services. Included in investment requirements are additions to the stock of producer durables, new construction, and changes in inventories.

How the value added approach treats investment goods can be illustrated as follows. Suppose that packaging equipment is fabricated in Cincinnati and shipped to Phoenix, where frozen carrots are packaged before being marketed nationally. The value added by the producer-durable industry in Cincinnati would appear as exports from Cincinnati, not from Phoenix. A community importing the frozen carrots would actually be importing the packaging equipment from Cincinnati, a certain amount of food processing from Phoenix, and transportation and related services from wherever they are based.

The value added by the construction industry in building facilities related to export activities such as factories, office buildings, or hotels are treated in the same way as producer durables—as exports from the place where the value is added. Ideally, residential construction should be treated as a part of local requirements. An attempt was made experimentally to adjust the data to high levels of construction. Modifications in the value added approach were devised to account for these variations, but with the necessary data available for one year only, 1960, the approach could not be elaborated. Accordingly, high levels of residential construction as well as other construction appear as exports from the metropolitan area in question.

It may also be noted that goods and services required by the construction industry will be underestimated in areas with above-average levels of construction activity and overestimated in areas with below-average levels of construction activity. Accordingly, trade in goods and services used in construction will be overestimated if they are produced locally, as sand and gravel normally are, and underestimated if, as in the case of steel and timber products, they are generally imported. The effect on aggregate trade activity or industry trade trends, however, should not be great.

The last type of investment considered is changes in inventories. In 1960, this category accounted for 5 percent of gross investment.[10] What should be noted is that production in a local industry in excess of local requirements will be classified as exports. What are classified as exports may not have been shipped; they may have been added to inventory by the local manufacturer. If they are shipped at a later date, they will not appear as exports at that time. On the other hand, they may have been shipped but not consumed, in which case there will have been inventory accumulations in the pipeline.

In summary, investment goods and services, with the exception of value added in residential construction, may, in fact, be traded; hence, requirements need not be met locally. Given the similarity of the local requirements of metropolitan areas for consumer and government goods and services, the industrial composition of investment goods consumed (in the form of final goods) will also tend to be similar and so will be their replacements (of capital stock). To complete the analysis, we have only to assume that net additions to the capital stock of investment goods represent a fixed proportion of total investment requirements in each community. In areas for which the requirements-mix assumption holds, the industrial composition of the national income will be a reliable estimator of the industrial composition of metropolitan requirements.

It must be recognized that this handling of investment goods comprises a weakness in the procedure. Where growth is rapid, unusual construction activity (residential and commercial) shows up as construction export. On the other hand, imports of durable equipment do not appear in the estimates of imports for the metropolis but are distributed throughout the national economy's requirements.

THE LOCALIZED NATURE OF PRIVATE HOUSEHOLD SERVICES

The basic premise of the value added approach, that in each industry local requirements and production are brought into balance by metropolitan trade, seems inappropriate for private households. A community would be importing private household services if nonresidents commuted to work there. Similarly, a community would export these services if residents commuted to work outside. In fact, it is unlikely that many private-household workers commute between metropolitan labor markets. It therefore seems advisable to treat all those employed in private households as meeting local requirements.

ESTIMATING EXPORTS AND IMPORTS AND CONVERTING TO EMPLOYMENT EQUIVALENTS

Trade activity is calculated for each metropolitan area by subtracting estimated requirements (in value added terms) in each industry from the production (again in value added terms) by that industry. When production exceeds requirements the difference is regarded as metropolitan exports; where it falls short of requirements, as metropolitan imports.

Although production requirements and trade are first estimated in dollar-value terms, in the chapters that follow they are expressed in employment terms—that is they are converted to employment equivalents by dividing by VAPE.

There are two reasons for this treatment. First, the principal objective of the study is to analyze the employment effects of trade. In each community, trade is assumed to be balanced in value added terms (that is, total requirements equal total production, and excesses of production in some industries are balanced by deficiencies in others). But in employment terms this is not the case. Employment terms of trade, defined as the ratio of employment equivalents of imports to those of exports, differ among metropolitan areas and they differ greatly between metropolitan and non-metropolitan places. Further, they change with growth and development. Secondly, the use of employment rather than value-added estimates makes possible interindustry and interdecade adjustments without price corrections.

A BRIEF MATHEMATICAL SUMMARY

The value added method can be summarized by the mathematical formulas presented below, which illustrate the calculations for any given

22

metropolitan area.* For metropolitan area j (Mj) the value added in production in industry i (VA_i) is estimated by applying the national index of value added per employee in the industry ($VAPE_i$) to employment in the industry (E_i) in Mj.

$$(1) \quad VA_i = VAPE_i \ (E_i) \quad i = 1_{j}31$$

Metropolitan income in place j (MI_j) is estimated by summing up the value added in production in all industries:

$$(2) \quad MI_j = \begin{matrix} i = K \\ [VA_i \\ i = I \end{matrix} \quad k = \text{number of industries} = 31$$

Metropolitan income is used as a proxy for metropolitan outlays (MO_j), a budget constraint on metropolitan expenditures for consumption and investment goods and services. It is assumed that there is no net flow of funds into or out of the area.

$$(3) \quad MO_j = MI_j$$

Metropolitan outlays are allocated among industries in the same proportions as national income except in the private households category, where requirements (MR_{PH}) are assumed to equal production. Metropolitan requirements from industry i (MR_i) are derived by applying the income allocation coefficient for the industry (IA_i)—share of national income excluding private household industry contributed by industry i—to total metropolitan outlays.

$$(4) \quad MR_i = IA_i \ (MO_j - MR_{PH}); \quad MR_{PH} \equiv VA_{PH}$$

Value added in production and metropolitan requirements in each industry are brought into balance through trade (T_i). Surplus production is attributed to exports. Deficiencies in production are assumed to be met by imports.

$$(5) \quad T_i = VA_i - MR_i \ \text{(Negative value of trade indicates imports.)}$$

The last step is to convert the trade statistic, which is in terms of value added, to employment terms. This is done by dividing T_i (value added terms) by the national index ($VAPE_i$).

$$(6a) \quad \text{Employment in exports}_i = \frac{\text{Positive values of } T_i}{VAPE_i}$$

*The general reader may want to skip this section and go directly to the summary and conclusions at the end of this chapter.

23

$$(6b) \quad \text{Employment in imports}_i = \frac{\text{Negative value of } T_i}{\text{VAPE}_i}$$

SUMMARY AND CONCLUSIONS

The procedure for estimating trade involves three basic steps. (1) *Estimation of production*. Here employment data are adjusted by applying VAPE estimates separately for each industrial classification. (2) *Estimation of requirements*. In each metropolis aggregate income is assumed to equal aggregate value of production, and this aggregate income defines the dollar amount of requirements. Requirements are allocated among industry categories for the metropolis in the same proportions as national income division studies have shown them to be allocated among industry categories for the nation as a whole. (3) *Estimation of trade*. Exports and imports are estimated by subtracting requirements in each industry from production in that industry. Excesses of production over requirements are assumed to be exported; deficiencies to be imported. Trade and local requirement estimates are then converted from value added to employment equivalents in order to permit analysis of the manpower effects of the development of trade.

The principal assumptions upon which this estimation procedure is based are that the national economy is a closed economy (there are no net exports or net imports), that each metropolis has a balance of imports and exports in value added terms (there are no flows of investment funds), that investment goods (including inventory accumulations) are embodied in the requirements for final goods and services of the metropolitan and non-metropolitan places of the entire national economy, and that the VAPE in an industry is equal to the national average in every metropolitan area.

Although there are theoretical weaknesses, especially in the handling of investment, the procedure does permit adjustment of production for value added and an estimation of requirements, which in other respects appear to give a good approximation of reality. This procedure permits measures of imports and exports, which make it possible to observe changes in metropolitan trade activity that could not be measured using earlier techniques.

NOTES

1. Employment data used in this study are census estimates published in Lowell D. Ashby, *Growth Patterns in Employment by County, 1940-1950 and 1950-1960*, 8 vols. (Washington, D.C.: U.S. Department of Commerce, 1965), XIV.

2. For a definition of an SMSA, see *Standard Metropolitan Statistical Areas*, U.S. Bureau of the Budget (Washington, D.C., 1965).

3. See Richard V. Knight, "Employment Expansion and Metropolitan Trade" (unpublished Ph.D. dissertation, London School of Economics and Political Science, University of London, 1972) for a discussion of earlier attempts to estimate trade and a bibliography of the literature.

4. Both employment and value added are reported annually for 64 industry classifications by the U.S. Department of Commerce. See *National Income and Product Accounts of the U.S., 1929-1965*, U.S. Department of Commerce, Office of Business Economics (Washington, D.C., 1966); "National Income by Industry," Table 1.12, pp. 18-21; "Number of Persons Engaged in Production," Table 6.6, pp. 110-13.

5. *Growth and Labor Characteristics of Manufacturing Industries*, U.S. Department of Commerce, Area Development Administration (Washington, D.C., October 1964), p. 4.

6. *Ibid.*, p. 5.

7. Solomon Fabricant, *A Primer on Productivity* (New York: Random House, 1969), p. 4.

8. Harvey S. Perloff, "Interrelations of State Income and Industrial Structure," *Review of Economics and Statistics* 39, 2 (May 1957), 162-71. Cited in H. S. Perloff, S. E. Dunn, E. E. Lampard, and R. F. Muth, *Regions, Resources, and Economic Growth* (Baltimore: The Johns Hopkins Press, 1960).

9. Frank Hanna, *State Income Differentials, 1919-1954* (Durham, N.C.: University Press, 1959), chapters 6 and 10, cited in Perloff, *et al.*, *Regions, Resources, and Economic Growth*.

10. *Business Statistics*, U.S. Department of Commerce, Office of Business Economics (Washington, D.C.: G.P.O., 1965) p. 8.

CHAPTER

3

A CASE STUDY:
HUNTSVILLE, ALABAMA

As a demonstration of the ways in which trade extimates may be used to shed light on economic growth, the value added approach has been applied to one metropolitan labor market—Huntsville, Alabama.[1] Admittedly, Huntsville is only one of the 368 metropolitan areas considered in this analysis of metropolitan trade. To study metropolitan trade trends and the role of trade in metropolitan growth, one is forced to use aggregated data. But probing one case can facilitate an understanding of the aggregated data.

Huntsville was chosen not at random, but on account of the contrasting growth characteristics during two succeeding decades—moderate growth in the 1940s and rapid growth with considerable industrial transition during the 1950s. Huntsville should thus afford a fair test of the appropriateness of the measures used to describe trade and analyze growth. If the measures are adequate in areas having moderate or rapid growth and extensive transition, they should be broadly applicable.

Huntsville in 1960 bears little resemblance to Huntsville in 1940. A small, rural, sleepy-eyed Southern textile town was transformed into the site of the George C. Marshall Space Flight Center, where rockets for manned space flights are assembled for the National Aeronautics and Space Administration (NASA). Not only was the new federal agency located there, but most of the assembly work, including construction of the first giant Saturn V rocket, was contracted out by NASA to private firms in the area. Proximity to the space center was important and many new industries developed in the vicinity of the NASA facility.

This transformation took place almost entirely during the 1950s. In that decade net employment increased by 20,495 (from 32,916 to 53,411). This compares to a net increase of only 5,692 jobs in the previous decade. The increased number of people employed does not tell the entire story; in fact, employment in export activity increased by only 600 jobs in the 1950s. But

26

average productivity increased very rapidly as employment in the older (low-VAPE) export industries was replaced by employment in the new (high-VAPE) export industries. Diversification, or broadening of the industrial base, and the upgrading of employment in the export sector gave impetus to a considerable expansion in the local sector.

TRADE IN HUNTSVILLE AT THREE POINTS IN TIME

Summary data relating to trade activity in Huntsville at three points in time are presented in Table 3.1. In 1940, export activity was limited in two industries—agriculture, which accounted for 81 percent of employment in export activity, and textiles, which accounted for the remaining 19 percent. These industries clearly dominated the export sector.

In 1940, Huntsville's economy was extremely specialized or "unbalanced." Imports were required in 27 of the 30 industry categories. In 20 of these industries over 25 percent of local requirements were imported; in 13, over 50 percent of local requirements were imported; and in 6, over 90 percent were imported. In general, service industries were more balanced than goods industries, which accounted for 67 percent of all imports in 1940. It is interesting to note that production and requirements were in balance in only one industry, food and dairy product stores.

Huntsville in 1950 closely resembled Huntsville in 1940. Changes that had occurred had only a marginal impact on the over-all structure of the economy. These changes did, however, signal a change in the general orientation of the Huntsville economy. Agricultural and textile exports still dominated the export sector (94.5 percent of export activity), but total employment in that sector declined as a result of decreased export activity in the two dominant export industries. The most significant development in the Huntsville economy in the 1940s was an increased diversification in the export sector; four industry categories were added. The emergence of these industries into export status indicated that Huntsville was becoming more than a one-industry town. A new manufacturing industry, chemicals and allied products, became a net exporter, thus broadening the manufacturing base, and three services appear in the net export column—an indication that Huntsville had begun to export services, probably to surrounding areas. The only industry in which a balance between imports and exports existed was trucking and warehousing.

By 1960, the NASA space center with its associated industries and military installations had attained a dominant position in the economy, and, concomitantly, agricultural and textile exports had declined precipitously. Employment in space-center-related exports accounted for approximately two-thirds of employment attributable to export activity in 1960; agriculture and textiles, which had so completely dominated this sector 20 years earlier, accounted for only 29.3 percent of export activity.

It should be noted that the many industries associated with the space center are not broken down individually; they fall into "other transportation

27

TABLE 3.1

Metropolitan Trade in Huntsville, Alabama
(employment equivalents)

Industry	Imports (percent distribution)			Exports (percent distribution)			Percent of Requirements Imported		
	1940	1950	1960	1940	1950	1960	1940	1950	1960
Primary									
Agriculture	0.3	0.1		81.3	72.6	21.6			
Forestry, fisheries							35.7	8.8	4.2
Mining	6.3	5.9	4.5				89.3	95.6	91.8
Construction	2.2	1.4				7.7	16.7	6.0	
Manufacturing									
Food, kindred products	5.0	4.9	5.6				58.4	52.4	41.6
Textile mills				18.7	16.9	2.6			
Apparel manufacturing	6.0	6.0	5.8				97.2	84.9	67.1
Lumber manufacturing	1.9	2.4	5.5				26.1	30.2	68.9
Printing, publishing	3.0	3.8	4.9				61.2	65.9	57.6
Chemicals, allied	2.6				0.4	0.2	75.3		
Electrical, other machinery	7.9	11.4	11.0				95.8	82.3	48.4
Motor vehicles, equipment	4.3	5.3	6.1				97.8	92.1	97.8
Other transportation equipment	2.4	3.1				4.9	99.2	92.3	
Other miscellaneous manufacturing	25.3	18.6				42.7	91.5	59.0	

	(5,136)	(7,011)	(10,345)	(13,941)	(12,803)	(13,403)			
Utilities	1.3	2.3	2.9				31.6	44.8	43.8
Mainly Business Services									
Railroad, railway express	6.2	6.8	5.7				70.7	73.8	81.8
Trucking, warehousing	0.6	2.1	2.4				15.0	35.8	35.8
Other transportation	2.0	1.1	3.4				47.4	35.8	51.3
Communications	1.8	4.1	1.2				59.0	23.3	19.4
Wholesale	2.9	5.3	7.4				30.8	31.2	45.0
FIRE	5.8		10.1				51.3	41.6	50.5
Business, repair services	0.4	0.9	2.9				6.7	10.1	24.1
Mainly Consumer Services					1.4	0.5			
Food, dairy stores	2.8	3.1	3.4				32.4	27.2	25.4
Eating, drinking places	0.5				0.8	0.8	1.8		
Other retail	1.9	0.5	1.4				14.6	4.1	9.6
Hotel, other personal services	1.4	1.2	1.6				44.9	35.7	42.0
Entertainment, recreation							4.2	11.1	25.1
Medical, other professions	1.1	3.5	14.2						
Government					2.9	1.4			
Public administration	1.8						15.6		
Armed forces	2.4	6.1				17.7	100.0	89.1	
All Industries	100.0	100.0	100.0	100.0	100.0	100.0	27.9	25.9	20.6
(Number)	(5,136)	(7,011)	(10,345)	(13,941)	(12,803)	(13,403)			

Source: Based on estimates of trade made by using the value added approach described in text (Chapter 2). Employment data used are census estimates published in Lowell D. Ashby, *Growth Patterns in Employment by County, 1940-1950 and 1950-1960,* 8 vols. (Washington, D.C.: U.S. Department of Commerce, 1965), xiv. See Table 3.2 for source of value added data.

equipment" and a residual category, "other and miscellaneous manufacturing." Thus, the diversification of the economy in terms of the number of industries represented in the export sector is understated in the analysis. Nevertheless, even with such limited industrial detail, we see that the export sector was diversified from 2 to 10 industries over these two decades.

The local sector was also diversified in the sense that the number of industries in which local production was deficient declined. Of the 28 industries that were net importers in 1940, 8 had become net exporters by 1960. In the goods sector (primary, construction, and manufacturing) 4 of the 12 categories that were net importers in 1940 had become net exporters. Further analysis of trade in those 19 industries remaining importers in 1960 revealed that in 9 the percent of local requirements that had to be imported declined. Over-all, while Huntsville was importing 28 percent of its local requirements in 1940, it was importing only 21 percent in 1960.

Despite the general trend toward greater diversification and self-sufficiency, there are segments of the Huntsville economy that did not expand rapidly enough to keep pace with local demand. Of the 28 importing industries in 1960, 9 had to import a greater percentage of local requirements in 1960 than in 1940. These industries were mining, lumber manufacturing, the three transportation categories, utilities, wholesaling, business services, and medical and other professional services.

One possible explanation for the increased dependence on imports, particularly in the service categories, is shortages of capital to construct and/or labor to staff the facilities required by a rapidly growing community. An above-average level of activity in the construction industry, reflected in the 7.7 percent "export" figure, suggests that the community's physical plant was being expanded at the time the 1960 census was taken.

Importing industries represent potential growth points, but this potential may be difficult to realize. Of particular interest is the fact that Huntsville imports over half of its requirements in printing and publishing and FIRE and is increasingly dependent on imports of business and repair services. The presence of such producer services would facilitate the establishment of new firms and the expansion of existing firms. Deficiencies in these producer services often deter growth. Reduction of these deficiencies (import substitution) would not only facilitate growth; it would indicate that Huntsville was evolving into a diversified service center, a place able to offer a wider range of externalized economies associated with rapid growth.[2]

This sketch of Huntsville at three points in time illustrates the usefulness of trade data in describing a metropolitan economy. The real significance of the approach for manpower analysis is derived, however, from the decadal analyses that follow, especially from the analysis of job increases and decreases.

DECADAL CHANGES IN TRADE

During the decade 1940-50, employment expansion in Huntsville was below the average for the nation (21 percent versus 27 percent in the nation). Metropolitan income, however, grew at a rate 61 percentage points above national income, and, over the same period, average VAPE in Huntsville rose from 66 to 81 percent of the national average. The relative rise is ascribed primarily to the loss of jobs in low-VAPE industries and to the addition of jobs in industries with higher VAPE. VAPE in industries in which jobs were destroyed was 54 percent below national levels in 1940; in contrast, average VAPE in industries in which jobs were created was only 4 percent below the 1950 national averages. This indicates a considerable upgrading of the city's economic base.

The upgrading process was conspicuous in the export sector. Average VAPE in export activity rose 241 percent, from 47 to 66 percent of the national average. Thus, even though employment in export activity declined by 1,138 jobs, the value of exports increased to such an extent as to allow imports to increase by the equivalent of 1,875 jobs. Average VAPE for imports dropped slightly over the decade from 127 to 121 percent of the national average.

In the analysis of trade change, the components of change—production, requirements, imports and exports—are referred to in terms of employment equivalents. Each component is further broken down into increasing and decreasing segments. These series are summarized in Table 3.2 and 3.3.

During the decade of the 1940s employment in production increased in all but 4 of the 31 industry categories, job increases totaling 7,729. Three-quarters of the 2,037 job decreases were in agriculture; the rest were in textiles (319), private household (176), and mining (20). Net employment increased by 5,692. Requirements increased in all but the agriculture and private households categories during the decade. Imports increased in 19 of the 27 industries that were net importers in 1940—that is, increases in local requirements exceeded those in production. Imports declined in the remaining 8 industries since increases in production exceeded requirements. Four of these industries became net exporters; production increased to such an extent that it surpassed local requirements. Agricultural production declined, reflecting declines in both exports and local requirements. In textiles a decline in production and increased local requirements resulted in decreased exports.

During the decade 1950-60 employment in Huntsville expanded at a rate four times the national average (by 62.3 percent compared to 15.6 percent in the nation). Average VAPE also continued to rise relative to the national average, from 81 percent to 93 percent. Metropolitan income (in current dollars) more than tripled in the 10-year period. The process of industrial transition and diversification that began in the previous decade quickened.

Net employment increased by 20,495 jobs in the 1950s (compared to 5,692 in the 1940s) to a total of 53,411 in 1960. Employment increases, numbering 29,338 jobs, occurred in 26 industries. Only five industries experienced employment declines, totaling 8,843 jobs. Of the declines, 79 percent were in agriculture and 19 percent in textiles.

Local requirements increased in all industries, but only in six were they exceeded by increases in production. Five of these six industries were net

31

TABLE 3.2

Imports and Exports in Metropolitan Labor Markets, Huntsville, Alabama

Industry	Employment (actual)			VAPE (dollars)		
	1940	1950	1960	1940	1950	1960
Primary						
Agriculture	14,690	13,168	6,170	*762	*2,602	*3,582
Forestry, fisheries	27	53	68	821	2,592	3,455
Mining	39	19	42	2,002	5,439	7,777
Construction	709	1,519	3,970	1,334	3,501	*5,787
Manufacturing						
Food, kindred products	183	315	819	1,971	4,220	6,717
Textile mills	3,062	2,743	1,087	*1,236	*3,493	*4,831
Apparel manufacturing	9	75	294	1,231	2,851	3,943
Lumber manufacturing	276	388	255	1,261	3,371	4,774
Printing, publishing	98	137	372	2,157	4,524	6,784
Chemicals, allied	43	364	689	3,154	*7,713	*10,982
Electrical, other machinery	18	172	1,215	2,644	5,085	7,503
Motor vehicles, equipment	5	33	14	2,939	8,207	11,883
Other transportation equipment	1	6	1,407	2,702	4,629	*7,650
Other miscellaneous manufacturing	120	910	10,052	2,192	5,420	*8,106
Utilities	147	203	388	4,122	7,007	14,226
Mainly Business Services						
Railroad, railway express	132	170	132	2,534	5,151	8,065
Trucking, warehousing	171	330	450	1,747	4,015	6,549
Other transportation	113	254	332	2,316	4,928	7,032
Communications	65	255	508	2,560	4,602	4,853
Wholesale	332	637	937	2,233	5,108	7,484
FIRE	285	525	1,027	5,153	10,899	16,593
Business, repair services	321	551	940	1,584	3,429	5,441
Mainly Consumer Services						
Food, dairy stores	595	991	1,364	1,472	*3,379	*4,481
Eating, drinking places	301	576	1,035	1,472	3,379	4,481
Other retail	1,459	2,522	4,800	1,472	*3,379	*4,481
Hotel, other personal services	573	834	1,351	1,062	2,420	3,485
Entertainment, recreation	87	149	225	1,800	3,121	4,654
Private households	1,595	1,419	2,737	555	1,504	2,379
Medical, other professions	1,269	1,994	4,367	1,798	3,330	5,062
Government						
Public administration	498	1,546	2,654	1,430	*3,001	*5,334
Armed forces		53	3,708	1,067	3,114	*4,269
All Industries	27,224	32,916	53,411	1,673	4,078	6,297
Rate of Increase		20.9	62.3		143.8	54.4

Note: Value of exports equals value of imports: 1940 = $12 million, 1950 = $36 million, 1960 = $82 million. Asterisk (*) indicates exports. (See Table 3.1.)

Source: Based on trade estimates made by using value added approach described in Chapter 2. Employment data are census estimates published in Lowell D. Ashby, *Growth Patterns in Employment by County, 1940-1950 and 1950-1960*, 8 vols. (Washington, D.C.:

Value of Output (dollars—millions)			Requirements (dollars—millions)			Exports (+) Imports (−) (dollars—millions)		
1940	1950	1960	1940	1950	1960	1940	1950	1960
11.19	34.26	22.10	2.55	8.42	11.74	8.64	25.85	10.36
0.02	0.14	0.24	0.04	0.15	0.25	−0.01	−0.01	−0.01
0.08	0.11	0.32	0.73	2.37	3.92	−0.65	−2.26	−3.59
0.95	5.32	22.97	1.10	5.66	17.00	−0.15	−0.34	5.97
0.36	1.33	5.50	0.87	2.79	9.43	−0.51	−1.46	−3.92
3.78	9.58	5.25	0.57	2.03	3.55	3.22	7.56	1.70
0.01	0.22	1.16	0.39	1.42	3.52	−0.38	−1.20	−2.36
0.35	1.31	1.22	0.47	1.88	3.92	−0.12	−0.57	−2.71
0.21	0.62	2.52	0.54	1.81	5.96	−0.33	−1.19	−3.44
0.14	2.81	7.57	0.55	2.38	7.31	−0.41	0.43	0.26
0.05	0.88	9.11	1.13	4.96	17.65	−1.08	−4.08	−8.54
0.01	0.27	0.17	0.67	3.34	7.70	−0.66	−3.07	−7.53
	0.03	10.76	0.33	1.05	5.75	−0.33	−1.02	5.01
0.26	4.93	81.49	3.11	12.02	35.14	−2.85	−7.08	46.34
0.61	1.42	5.52	0.89	2.57	9.84	−0.28	−1.15	−4.32
0.34	0.88	1.07	1.15	3.34	5.84	−0.81	−2.47	−4.78
0.30	1.33	2.95	0.35	1.32	4.60	−0.05	0.01	−1.65
0.26	1.28	2.34	0.30	1.99	4.80	−0.24	−0.71	−2.47
0.17	1.17	5.01	0.40	1.53	6.22	−0.24	−0.36	−1.21
0.74	3.25	7.01	1.07	4.73	12.75	−0.33	−1.48	−5.74
1.47	5.72	17.04	3.01	9.79	34.43	−1.54	−4.07	−17.39
0.51	1.89	5.12	0.55	2.11	6.75	−0.04	−0.22	−1.63
0.88	3.35	6.11	0.87	2.72	5.83	—	0.62	0.28
0.44	1.95	4.64	0.66	2.67	6.22	−0.21	−0.73	−1.58
2.15	8.52	21.51	2.10	8.19	21.01	−0.04	0.33	0.50
0.61	2.02	4.71	0.71	2.11	5.21	−0.10	−0.09	−0.50
0.16	0.46	1.05	0.28	0.72	1.80	−0.13	−0.26	−0.76
0.89	2.13	6.51	0.89	2.13	6.51	—	—	—
2.28	6.64	22.11	2.38	7.47	29.54	−0.10	−0.83	−7.43
0.71	4.95	14.16	0.84	3.76	13.15	−0.13	1.19	1.00
	0.17	15.83	0.13	1.49	5.70	−0.13	−1.33	10.13
29.92	108.91	313.06	29.92	108.91	313.06	—	—	—
	264.0	187.4	264.0	187.4				

U.S. Department of Commerce, 1965). Value added per employee based on data published in U.S. Department of Commerce, Office of Business Economics, *National Income and Product Accounts of the U.S., 1929-1965* (Washington, D.C.: 1966), National Income by Industry, Table 1.12, pp. 18-21. Number of Persons Engaged in Production, Table 6.6, pp. 110-113.

TABLE 3.3

Analysis of Job Creation and Job Destruction by Industry in Huntsville, Alabama

Industry	Decade 1940-50, Percent of Job Increase (Decrease)					Decade 1950-60, Percent of Job Increase (Decrease)				
	Job Increase Decrease (−) (actual)	Import Decrease (Increase) (%)	Export Increase (Decrease) (%)	Local Demand Increase (Decrease) (%)	Import Subst. (%)	Job Increase Decrease (−) (actual)	Import Decrease (Increase) (%)	Export Increase (Decrease) (%)	Local Demand Increase (Decrease) (%)	Import Subst. (%)
Primary										
Agriculture	−1,522		(92.4)	(7.6)		−6,998		(100.0)	86.7	20.0
Forestry, fisheries	26	40.0		60.0	60.0	15	13.3		100.0	86.4
Mining	−20	(100.0)				23				
Construction	810	2.0		98.0	15.4	2,451	4.0	42.1	54.0	
Manufacturing										
Food, kindred products	132			100.0	29.5	504		(100.0)	100.0	29.8
Textile mills	−319		(100.0)			−1,656		(100.0)		
Apparel manufacturing	66			100.0	90.9	219			100.0	72.9
Lumber manufacturing	112			100.0		−133	(100.0)			
Printing, publishing	39			100.0		235			100.0	30.2
Chemicals, allied	321	40.9	17.2	41.9	66.9	325			100.0	
Electrical, other machinery	154			100.0	84.4	1,043			100.0	76.6
Motor vehicles, equipment	28			100.0	85.2	−19	(100.0)			
Other transportation equipment	5			100.0	80.0	1,401	15.6	46.7	37.6	43.6
Other miscellaneous manufacturing	790			100.0	91.4	9,142	14.3	62.5	23.2	17.3

34

Utilities	56			100.0		185		100.0	100.0	
Mainly Business Services										
Railroad, railway express	38			100.0	10.7	−38	(100.0)			
Trucking, warehousing	159	18.9	0.6	80.5	31.7	120			100.0	
Other transportation	146			100.0	61.6	73			100.0	
Communications	190	7.9		92.1		253			100.0	9.5
Wholesale	305			100.0		300			100.0	
FIRE	240			100.0		502			100.0	
Business, repair services	230			100.0	36.0	389			100.0	
Mainly Consumer Services										
Food, dairy stores	396		46.6	53.4		373			100.0	
Eating, drinking places	275			100.0	14.6	459			100.0	5.2
Other retail	1,063		9.1	88.3		2,278	0.6		99.4	
Hotel, other personal services	261	23.8		76.2	35.0	517			100.0	
Entertainment, recreation	62			100.0	32.8	76			100.0	
Medical, other professions	725			100.0		2,373			100.0	
Government										
Public administration	1,048	8.8	35.3	55.9		1,108	11.7		100.0	
Armed forces	53			100.0	98.1	3,655	64.9		23.4	2.1
All Industries	5,692	5.0	9.2	85.9	23.3	20,495	7.0	33.4	59.6	12.0
(Number)		(1.0)	(84.7)	(14.3)			(2.1)	(97.9)		

Source: Based on estimates of trade made by using the value added approach described in the text.

importers in 1950; four of them became net exporters during the decade—a shift that represents the reduction of imports by 2,051 jobs and an increase in exports of 9,775 jobs. In the other importing industry (mining), imports declined slightly and in the sixth (other retailing), an exporting industry, exports increased. In the remaining 24 industries, in which increased requirements exceeded production, imports were increased by 5,385 jobs in 19 and exports declined in 9,189 in 4.

Altogether, increased exports accounted for 9,789 new jobs in five industries. Gains were, however, almost entirely offset by declines. Declines in six industries numbered 9,189 jobs; as a result, there was a net increase of only 600 jobs in the export sector. Productivity of employment in the export sector continued to rise from 66 to 93 percent of the national average. The employment terms of trade (ETOT) also continued to improve; the ETOT ratio rose from 55 to 77 in 1960, and the difference between the employment equivalence of imports and exports declined 2,734 jobs.*

JOB-INCREASE-JOB-DECREASE ANALYSIS

Additional insights may be gained from the analysis of decadal changes in employment (production), requirements, and trade, by examining each component, industry by industry, to determine whether it contributed to job increases or job decreases (Table 3.3).**

The breakdown of job increases shows the importance of growth in the local sector. Higher levels of local consumption accounted for 86 percent of the growth in the first decade and 60 percent in the second decade. Expanded export activity accounted for one-third of the job increases in the

---

*The relationship between VAPE in imported and exported industries may best be expressed as the ratio of employment equivalents of imports to the number employed in export activity—the employment terms of trade. An ETOT ratio greater than 100 indicates that fewer men are required for $1 worth of exports than for $1 worth of imports. In 1940, the ETOT ratio in Huntsville was 37: It took 100 workers in Huntsville to produce exports having the same value as imports produced by 37 workers in other places. By 1950, the ETOT ratio had risen to 55. The significance of the terms of trade measure will be discussed in Chapter 5.

**In equations B1 and B2 below, the six components of change are arranged according to whether they contribute to or offset an increase or a decrease in employment, and employment changes are assessed with respect to the relative importance of contributing factors. For example, job increases in production in industry i (JI_i) may reflect increased exports if it is an exporting industry (XI_i), declining imports if it is (or was) an importing industry (MD_i), increased local requirements (RI_i), or some combination of the three factors. Since declining exports (XD_i), increased imports (MI_i), and declining requirements (RD_i) offset the increases, they must be subtracted from the contributing factors.

Similarly, job decreases in an industry (JD_i) may reflect decreased export activity (XD_i), increased imports (MI_i), decreased local requirements (RD_i), or some combination of these possibilities. The two general cases may be stated as follows:

$$(B1) \quad JI_i = XI_i + MD_i + RI_i - (XD_i + MI_i + RD_i)$$
$$(B2) \quad JD_i = XD_i + MI_i + RD_i - (XI_i + MD_i + RI_i)$$

36

1950s, but only 9 percent in the 1940s. Decreased imports played a minor role in Huntsville's growth, accounting for only 5 percent and 7 percent of the job increases in the respective decades.

MEASURING IMPORT SUBSTITUTION

A more sophisticated way to view the decline of import activity is to measure it in a relative fashion. Import declines simply refer to the direct replacement of imports by local production. If the period analyzed is of considerable duration, however, this definition may be too limiting, for it will fail to take into consideration the rise of requirements under conditions of growth. Decrease in the value of imports during the period will understate the full extent of import substitution that has occurred. It is for this reason that the best criteria for measuring import substitution is a relative rather than an absolute one. *Import substitution* is measured by any reduction in the *percent* of requirements imported, with the percent reduction in imports translated into employment equivalents.

The modified definition of import substitution appears useful. By this definition, the role of import substitution in Huntsville is more substantial than the simple decline in imports suggests. Import substitution was responsible for 23.3 percent of the job increases in the first decade and 12.0 percent of the increases in the second decade (Table 3.3). Import substitution was more important as a source of jobs in the 1940s, when few jobs opened up in the export sector, than in the 1950s, when many jobs were created in expanding export industries. Half of the job increases in both decades were in consumer and business service classifications. When growth was slow (in the 1940s) approximately 15 percent of these new service jobs were added in the process of import substitution; when growth was fast (in the 1950s), less than 1 percent of the new service jobs could be attributed to import substitution.

In both decades jobs destroyed can be traced primarily to declining export activity. Decreased exports, largely in the agriculture and textile categories, were responsible for 85 percent and 98 percent of the job decreases in the respective decades. In the 1940s, private households' employment decreased, but, as explained earlier, all changes in this category are attributed to changes in local demand and supply factors. There were four instances (three in the second decade) in which local production was replaced by increased imports. At any rate, the jobs lost through replacement of local production were not significant; they accounted for only 1 percent of the jobs destroyed in the 1940s and 2 percent of the jobs destroyed in the 1950s.

This analysis of job increases and job declines provides additional evidence to support the interpretation of Huntsville's growth presented earlier and sheds further light on the changing relationship between the export and local sectors. Increased self-sufficiency in the local sector and increased diversity and upgrading export activity have significantly changed the relationship between the two sectors. In 1940, there was approximately one job in the local sector for each job in the export sector; two decades later this ratio had changed from 1:1 to 3:1. If this ratio is stable over the short run, as some export-base theorists hypothesize, one may deduce that the local impact of employment changes in the export sector tripled. Whereas, for example, the addition (or loss) of 100 jobs in the export sector in 1940 would have induced 100 additional (fewer) jobs in the local sector, by 1960 the local impact would have been three times as great, involving 300 more (fewer) jobs in the local sector. The theoretical basis for this relationship—the export-base multiplier—is presented and the export-base hypothesis is tested in the next chapter.

IMPLICATIONS FOR HUNTSVILLE IN THE 1970s

Huntsville's spurt in growth was a direct result of the high priority given to the national space program aimed at placing a man on the moon. Location of the Saturn V rocket program in Huntsville was also a policy decision. Objectives of the program were met in 1969 when the astronauts completed their historic flights. By 1970, the reordering of national priorities was already taking effect. Substantial cutbacks were made in employment at the George C. Marshall Space Flight Center, and private firms began transferring or discharging many of their employees.[3] The space flight center in Huntsville is rapidly turning into a museum piece. It is symbolic that Dr. Werner von Braun, recently returned to Huntsville for the dedication of a huge new aerospace museum.

Huntsville, a "product" of the space program, became its "victim" and is now trying to attract new industries. It is reportedly vying for the Third Army Headquarters, which may be moved from Fort McPherson, just outside of Atlanta. The Third Army, with its 2,500 to 3,000 civilian jobs, would certainly help take up some of the slack in the Huntsville economy, but it would represent a downgrading of the export sector in terms of VAPE.

The analysis of Huntsville's trade activity points up two features of a community's growth that require emphasis. The first is that as a community develops, it becomes more diversified and the local impact of changes in export activity increases. But the amplification of changes in exports works in both directions; the community also becomes more vulnerable to cutbacks in export activity. Huntsville was particularly vulnerable because it was a one-government-program town. Almost the entire export sector was linked to the space flight center. Seattle suffered a similar fate when aircraft orders fell, costs were cut, and 55,000 people were laid off at Boeing. The initial cuts in late 1968 helped spur the Seattle economy by releasing men at a time when labor shortages were being experienced by many local businesses. But they absorbed all they could, and the situation turned sour. Unemployment rates have since reached 16 percent, and Seattle remains as of fall 1972 a city with severe unemployment problems. An interesting contrast to Huntsville and Seattle is Houston, where industrial diversification and rapid growth insulated the city from serious unemployment problems when its space program activities were cut back.

The second point is that national programs, such as space, often are geographically concentrated. A community whose export sector is dependent on the production of public goods is even more vulnerable to changes arising out of shifts in political priorities than communities such as Detroit or Pittsburgh, which are vulnerable to fluctuations in the demand for private goods. Government programs and policies play a critical role in the spatial organization of the national economy. Huntsville clearly demonstrates the impact that a particular government program may have on a particular location.

It should be possible to be sensitive to regional growth objectives in locating major government facilities such as a space flight center. If the facility is not to be permanent, it may be desirable to place it in a labor market large enough so that its opening or eventual closing will not be unduly disruptive to the local economy. If it is to be permanent, the facility might be located in a growth center where the benefits to be realized from increasing import substitution and the scale of production in the local sector (economies of scale) can be maximized.

NOTES

1. Detailed data for Huntsville can be found in Richard Knight, "Employment Expansion and Metropolitan Trade" (unpublished Ph.D. dissertation, London School of Economics and Political Science, University of London, 1972), Appendix B. Figures in this chapter are based on these detailed calculations.

2. Thomas M. Stanback and Richard V. Knight, *The Metropolitan Economy: The Process of Employment Expansion* (New York: Columbia University Press, 1970), pp. 152-54.

3. Conditions in Huntsville in 1970 are described in an article by James T. Wooten, "Conditions in Huntsville," in The *New York Times,* March 23, 1970.

CHAPTER

4

THE TRADE MULTIPLIER

The primary objective of this chapter is to explore the relationship between total employment and export activity in a metropolitan area. This relationship is generally specified in terms of a multiplier, defined as the ratio of total metropolitan employment to employment in the export sector. This multiplier is a simple concept and easy to calculate once trade activity has been estimated. A trade multiplier of 5 indicates that of every five jobs in the metropolitan economy, one is in the export sector.[1]

The mechanism by which the metropolitan trade multiplier (MTM) functions depends on certain characteristics of income flows and on the industrial composition of the local sector. Income flows may be conceptualized as follows: Exogenous income enters the metropolitan economy in payment for exports and is in turn distributed among the factors of production in the form of wages, rent, interest, profits, and payments for inputs of materials and services used in production. To the extent that consumption goods or services are imported or consumed outside the economy or production inputs are imported, a certain proportion of the export earnings will flow out of the economy. If consumption goods or services and production inputs are produced locally, income flows will remain within the community.

It is clear that the greater the range of goods and services produced and sold locally, the greater will be the share of payments that are recirculated within the community. Each successive cycle of income flowing through the local economy results in more payments to the local factors and further sustains employment in the local sector. The MTM, the ratio of total employment to employment in export activity, may thus be considered as the net result of the income flows once the system is in equilibrium. In that condition, the net annual inflow of funds accrued from exports equals the net annual outflow of funds for imports.*

---

*Here as in Chapter 2 we assume no inflow or outflow of investment funds.

The MTM is a summary statistic that facilitates useful observations about metropolitan economies. It indicates, first, the relative importance of the export sector in terms of the share of the labor force thus engaged, the proportion of employment in the export sector being the reciprocal of the multiplier.

The multiplier indicates, secondly, the degree of diversity or specialization that a metropolis has attained. A low MTM implies that a relatively small proportion of local requirements are produced locally and that production is specialized in a limited number of industrial categories. A high multiplier indicates a high level of self-sufficiency and suggests a relatively high level of industrial diversification.

Finally, the MTM is an indicator of the total impact that changes in export activity have on the economy. A low multiplier signifies a high degree of income leakages in the form of imports and thus indicates that increased export earnings have a low income-generating effect in the local community. A high multiplier indicates low leakages and a high income-generating effect.

VARIATION IN THE TRADE MULTIPLIER

The MTM varies over a wide range. Among the 368 cities observed at three different points in time, the range extended from 1.5 to 11.2.

The variation in the value of the MTM is explained in large part by three related factors—the size of the city's population, the VAPE in the city's export sector, and the industrial diversity of its export sector.

Size of place measured in terms of population affects the magnitude of the multiplier because larger areas can support a more diverse local sector. Goods or services that must be imported in small cities—such as packaging materials, printing, or legal services—can be produced locally in larger areas because market-size thresholds for efficient production are reached.

The influence of population size on the multiplier is evident in the data in Table 4.1. In all metropolitan places combined, the average multiplier was 4.6, but it increased from 4.1 in small cities to 5.3 in medium-sized cities to 7.6 in large cities. This relationship is the same for all types of cities with the single exception of the large government category, which represents Washington, D.C. For example, the average multiplier in nodal cities rises from 4.5 in small areas to 6.4 in medium-sized to 7.7 in large cities; in manufacturing cities the respective figures are 4.3, 5.1, and 7.1.

Differences in VAPE in the export sector affect the magnitude of the trade multiplier as follows: High VAPE in export activity implies a high average level of demand for goods and services produced in the local sector. It is expected that, to meet this relatively high level of demand, there will be more jobs in the local sector than if value added levels were lower. It is hypothesized, therefore, that the metropolitan trade multiplier will be above (below) average in places with above (below) average levels of value added in export activity.

41

TABLE 4.1

Metropolitan Trade Multiplier by
Type and Size Category of Place*
(mean values, 1960)

Type of Place	Small	Medium	Large	All Metro Places
Nodal	4.5 (30)	6.4 (30)	7.7 (6)	5.7 (66)
Manufacturing	4.3 (70)	5.1 (40)	7.1 (4)	4.7 (114)
Government	3.1 (30)	3.3 (14)	2.8 (1)	3.2 (45)
Medical-educational	3.4 (19)	3.9 (2)	—	3.4 (21)
Resort	3.2 (6)	3.6 (2)	—	3.3 (8)
Mixed	4.4 (47)	5.6 (12)	11.2 (1)	4.8 (60)
Mixed with nodal characteristics	4.4 (39)	6.2 (14)	10.3 (1)	5.0 (54)
All metropolitan places	4.1 (241)	5.3 (114)	7.6 (13)	4.6 (368)

*Number of places in category are placed in parentheses. The types of place are those discussed earlier. Detailed definitions can be found in Thomas M. Stanback and Richard V. Knight, *The Metropolitan Economy: The Process of Employment Expansion* (New York: Columbia University Press, 1970), pp. 132-37.

Size of MLMs is based on 1960 population. Small-size MLMs: SMSAs with 50,001-200,000 population plus non-SMSA counties with a city of 25,000 or more in 1960. Medium-size MLMs: SMSAs with 200,001-1,600,000 population. Large-size MLMs: SMSAs with 1,600,001 or more population.

Source: Based on estimates of trade made by using the value added approach described in the text. See Table 3.2.

The relationship between a city's VAPE and the size of its multiplier is apparent in the data in Table 4.2.* While it is difficult to assess the significance of statistical tests involving relatively few observations (7), the Spearman rank-order correlation coefficient for the two sets of figures is high (.75). Even without the statistical tests, the reader can observe the close relationship that holds between the value of the multiplier and VAPE. Except for manufacturing cities, which often have high VAPE but a more

*A metropolitan area's productivity (VAPEM)—that is its total average VAPE, is largely a function of the productivity of its export sector (VAPEX). The relationship is expressed in the following regression equation: $VAPEM^k = \$3,961 + .33(VAPEX^k)$; K = 1,368; (standard error of estimate = 175.3, F ratio = 3120.9, R^2 = .8950).

TABLE 4.2

Average VAPE and Average MTM by Type of Place, 1960

Type of Place	Multiplier	VAPE*
Nodal	5.7 (1)	105.9 (2)
Mixed with nodal characteristics	5.0 (2)	102.0 (3)
Mixed	4.8 (3)	100.4 (4)
Manufacturing	4.7 (4)	108.7 (1)
Medical-educational	3.4 (5)	93.0 (6)
Resort	3.3 (6)	93.5 (5)
Government	3.2 (7)	91.3 (7)

*Expressed as a percent of average national VAPE.
Source: Based on estimates of trade made by using the value added approach described.

limited (relative to income generated) local sector, the ranking of cities in each column is very close.

The size of an area's multiplier is also related to the industrial diversity of its export sector. In general, it can be anticipated that the more diversity in the export sector, the less a metropolitan economy need rely on imports and the less income generated will be leaked out of the area to pay for such imports. In contrast, specialization in exports (which is most common in manufacturing-type places) should require greater imports, resulting in higher income leakages and lower trade multipliers.

The relationship between the MTM and the three variables described above—size of place, productivity in the export sector, and diversity of exports—was tested using data from 368 places in 1960. Size was measured in a log function of the number of employees in the metropolitan area (LOGME) to allow for the uneven distribution of this variable. Average income generated per employee in the export sector (VAPEX) was measured directly in terms of thousands of dollars. Diversity in the export sector was gauged by computing the percent of *total* employment in exporting industries (that is, those industries for which there was a positive difference between output and requirements), which was accounted for by export activity (PXIX).* The results of the regression analysis are as follows:

$$MTM = -0.466 -0.07 \ (PXIX) + .43 \ (VAPEX) + 1.0815 \ (LOGME)$$
$$(.003) \qquad\qquad (.03) \qquad\quad (.09)$$

*Thus if in a given metropolitan area five industries with a total of 20,000 employed are found to have export trade balances and the employment equivalent of the export balance is equal to 5,000, the PXIX ratio will be .25. It will seem that in general the more concentrated is export activity in one or a few activities the larger will be the share of their employment in export and the higher the PXIX.

$$\text{Standard error of estimate} = .8923, \text{ F ratio} = -427.561$$
$$R^2 = .7821$$

Together, the three variables accounted for 78 percent of the variance in the value of the multiplier. The values of the regression coefficients indicate that the expected relationships between the multiplier and each variable are correct and their standard errors (in parenthesis) indicate a high level of statistical reliability. The multiplier increased (that is, was positively correlated) with size and with VAPE in the export sector. Since PXIX decreases with diversity in the export sector, the negative regression coefficient confirms the hypothesized relationship.

THE CHANGING VALUE OF THE MULTIPLIER

One of the first questions to arise in discussions concerning the application of the multiplier concept to growth analysis is whether employment multipliers represent a short-term (a period ranging from a few weeks to a year) or a long-term relationship. In this study, the multiplier is used in the analysis of long-term (decadal) growth and not in the analysis of short-term adjustments.

The multiplier is best used in long-term analysis because it cannot adequately take into account the diverse factors that influence the short-run relationship between change in export activity and total employment. Insofar as marginal adjustments differ from normal production procedures the short-run multiplier is likely to differ from the average trade multiplier. If, on the other hand, sufficient time is allowed to elapse for appropriate changes to take place in the local sector, considerable expansion will occur in response to the initial stimulus. In this event, the marginal multiplier is more likely to approximate the average multiplier.

The stability of the multiplier can be tested by comparing the actual employment change at the end of a decade with an estimate of employment change obtained by applying the multiplier.* This test was performed using data from the 368 metropolitan areas for each of the two decades 1940-50 and 1950-60. In the calculations, rates of change are compared so that the results will not be biased by the skewed distribution of actual changes in employment. The results of the test are presented in Table 4.3 in the form of a regression equation in which the actual growth rate (E_R) equals a

---

*The formula for actual employment change is $\Delta E = E_t + 10 - E_t$; where E_t represents total employment at the beginning of the decade and E_{t+10} represents total employment at the end. The formula for estimated employment change is $\Delta E' = \Delta E_x K_t$, where ΔE_x represents change in export employment and K_t equals the trade multiplier at the beginning of the decade. This test differs from tests of the export-base hypothesis. We are testing the stability of the multiplier by correlating predicted change in employment assuming the multiplier constant with actual change in employment. Two prior analyses correlated change in the base-service ratio with population change. They sought (unsuccessfully) to show that an increased share of employment in the export sector results in increased population.[2]

TABLE 4.3

Test Results

Decade	a Constant	b Regression Coefficient	Standard Error	Correlation Coefficient	r^2	F Ratio
1940-50	12.48	0.59	(.014)	.91	.84	1863.6
1950-60	13.40	0.77	(.027)	.83	.68	824.4

Source: Based on estimates of trade made by using the value added approach described in the text. See Table 3.2.

constant (a) plus the product of a regression coefficient (b) and the estimated growth rate (E'_R).*

The actual and estimated values of employment change are found to be highly correlated in both decades. The correlation coefficient (r) is .91 for 1940-50 and .83 for 1950-60. These coefficients are statistically significant at the 99 percent confidence level. The value of the coefficient of determination (r^2) indicates that the equation "explains" 84 percent of the variation in the employment growth rates of metropolitan areas during the 1940s and 68 percent during the 1950s.

The regression results point to important conclusions about the stability and predictive value of the trade multiplier. First, the multiplier is not a static relationship. The relatively high intercept value (a) indicates a general increase in the value of the multiplier in all places in each of the two decades. That is, even if the estimated rate of change calculated by using the multiplier were zero (that is, no expansion in the export sector), total employment would have grown by 12 percent in the 1940s and 13 percent in the 1950s. This growth represents an increase in the value of the multiplier rather than expansion in the export sector. During the 1940s the intercept value of 12.48 represented about one-third of the mean growth rate of all metropolitan areas, and during the 1950s the intercept value of 13.40 represented almost two-thirds the mean growth. In brief, the high constant indicates the average value of the multiplier changed significantly over each of the decades.

The values of the regression parameters indicate that *change* in the value of the multiplier was a more important source of growth in slow-growing places

---

*The formulas for actual rate of change in employment (E_R) and estimated rate of change in employment (E_R') are

$$E_R = (E^{t+10} - E_t)/E_t$$
$$E_R' = [(E_x^{t+10} - E_x^t)(K^t)]/E^t$$

The regression equation is

$$E_R = a + bE_R'$$

45

than in fast-growing ones. In the example above, where growth in the export sector was zero, all growth is represented by change in the value of the multiplier (that is, the constant a). Compare this to a hypothetical city in which the export sector grew rapidly and in which employment change ($E_R{}^1$) calculated by using the multiplier is 50 percent for 1950-60. In this case the rate of change produced by the regression equation is [13.40 + .77 (.50) = 51.9], so the multiplier appears to have changed only minimally. However, in a case where the estimated growth according to the multiplier was 10 percent, the value produced by the regression equation would be 21.1 percent.

As noted earlier (Table 4.3), the values of r^2 indicate that the regression analysis was able to "explain" 84 percent and 68 percent of the variation in growth rates in the respective decades. While in both instances this is a relatively high percentage, the important point is the declining significance of the multiplier in predicting employment changes. Phrased another way, this means a trend toward an increasing value of the multiplier.

Over time, the MTM will change only if employment in the local and export sectors expands at different rates. This may happen when VAPE increases faster in the export sector than the local sector. The result will be an increase in income and investment funds and in the demand for goods and services of the local sector. Accordingly there will be a related rise in employment in the local sector and hence an increase in the MTM.

This is exactly what took place during both decades. With a general rise in incomes and a differential increase in productivity between goods and services, there was a disproportionate increase in employment in the local service sector. As will be shown in Chapter 5, employment increased rapidly in consumer services, largely because of increases in the medical-educational services category and, to a lesser extent, in retailing.

A similar result can come about from differential changes in VAPE in export and import industries. If productivity increases faster in industries exported than in those imported, the terms of trade become more favorable (See Chapter 5), the local economy becomes richer, and local demand improves. The trade multiplier increases.

An evaluation of the net effect that changes in VAPE for individual industry categories had on MTMs is difficult. During the 1940s, VAPE increased rapidly in industries in which metropolitan areas were net importers, such as agriculture and mining (See Table 2.1). While this would suggest a decline in MTMs, it was offset by a relative decline in metropolitan demand for the output of those same industries and by relatively high increases in VAPE in metropolitan export activity. It is not entirely clear which effects were dominant.

For the second decade the case is clearer. Changes in the average VAPE in net metropolitan imports were less than in net metropolitan exports. The conditions that tended to decrease the multiplier during the 1940s actually had the effect of increasing it during the 1950s. Furthermore, such conditions as low VAPE gains in the local sectors relative to gains in the export sector that tend to increase the multiplier were accentuated during the second decade.

The other factors that affect the stability of the MTM are structural changes that occur with the growth of a metropolitan area's population. The process of import substitution implies an increase, and the process of production replacement (increased imports), a decrease in the MTM. Import substitution is likely to be made possible as a city's population grows and economies of scale and industry thresholds are achieved, thus permitting local production of previously imported goods and services. The fact that import substitution (9 percent) and increased local requirements (76 percent) accounted for over four-fifths of the job increases in the 1950s (See Table 5.8) suggests that the net effect of these factors is an increase in the average value of the MTM.

SUMMARY

In this chapter we found that the relationship between employment in the export sector and total metropolitan employment (the trade multiplier) is neither uniform among cities nor constant over time. Trade multipliers varied widely among cities in 1940, 1950, and 1960. In addition, the size of a city's multiplier often changed significantly over the course of each decade. These changes, which are attributable to changes in national parameters and to structural changes that occur with metropolitan growth, were greater in the 1950s than the 1940s. The substantial, but declining, predictive value of the multiplier was evident in a regression analysis, which explained 84 percent of the variation in growth rates for the 1940s but only 68 percent for the 1950s.

The different relationships between export and local sectors among cities as well as the increase in MTMs over time appear to result from the same factors—size of place, VAPE in the export sector, and diversity of export activity. A regression analysis using these three variables was able to account for 88 percent of the variation in MTMs in 1960.

In conclusion, it is evident from the above analyses that economic base studies should make allowance for changes in national parameters and structural changes that occur with metropolitan growth, that is, the upgrading of the export sector, the loss of certain functions (production replacement), and the broadening of the local sector (import substitution).

NOTES

1. Urban planners frequently refer to the relationship in terms of a "base-service ratio." See Richard Andrews, "The Problem of Terminology," *Land Economics*, August 1953, pp. 263-68.

2. See Ralph W. Pfouts, "An Empirical Testing of the Economic Base Theory," *Journal of the American Institute of Planners* 23 (Spring 1957), pp. 64-69. Reprinted in Ralph W. Pfouts, ed., *The Techniques of Urban Economic Analysis* (West Trenton: Chandler-Davis, 1960); and R. W. Pfouts and E. T. Curtis, "Limitations of the Economic Base Analysis," *Social Forces*, no. 4 (May 1958), pp. 303-10. Reprinted in Pfouts, ed., *Techniques of Urban Economic Analysis*.

5

CHANGING PATTERNS
OF METROPOLITAN TRADE

This chapter analyzes the changing trade patterns within the American economy in the two decades 1940 to 1950 and 1950 to 1960 and relates these changes in trade to the process of employment expansion. After a necessary preliminary discussion of differentiated growth in metropolitan and non-metropolitan areas, estimates of the level of aggregate metropolitan trade are presented. These estimates are then divided into their industrial components and into trade among metropolitan areas and trade between metropolitan and non-metropolitan areas. In addition, trade estimates are presented for metropolitan areas by size of place and by type of place. Finally, we return to the aggregate metropolitan trade estimates to determine the relative importance of the various growth processes—change in export activity, change in local requirements, and decline in imports—in explaining metropolitan employment expansion.

METROPOLITAN AND NON-METROPOLITAN GROWTH TRENDS

Preliminary to the analysis of changing trade patterns it is useful to examine the general trends underlying metropolitan and non-metropolitan growth. National trends in VAPE demand and employment have had a differential impact on metropolitan and non-metropolitan areas. Rates of growth in value of output (demand), VAPE, and employment in metropolitan and non-metropolitan areas are presented for both decades in Table 5.1.

During the 1940s the value of output increased at about the same rate in both types of areas, but gains in VAPE in metropolitan counties were considerably lower than in non-metropolitan areas, with the result that employment expanded more slowly in non-metropolitan than in metropolitan areas, 12 percent compared to 34 percent.

TABLE 5.1

Growth Rates in Metropolitan and Non-metropolitan Areas
(percent)

Area	1940-50			1950-60		
	Value of Output	VAPE	Employment	Value of Output	VAPE	Employment
Metropolitan	+211	+132	+34	+86	+53	+21
Non-metropolitan	+204	+171	+12	+55	+54	+ 1
Nation	+197	+144	+27	+72	+54	+15

Source: Based on estimates of trade made by using value added approach described in text. See Table 3.2.

During the following decade, gain in VAPE was approximately the same in both types of areas, but value of output in the metropolitan areas increased at a rate over 50 percent higher than in the non-metropolitan areas, again with the result that employment expanded at a much faster rate in metropolitan than in non-metropolitan places. Employment in non-metropolitan areas increased only 1.3 percent from 1950 to 1960; only 121,800 net jobs were added outside of the metropolitan areas.

The differing growth characteristics of metropolitan and non-metropolitan areas can be explained in large part by the demand and VAPE changes of industries that are concentrated in the areas. An analysis of the distribution of employment in each of the industry categories (Table 5.2) indicates that the "most metropolitan" industries are motor vehicles (91 percent of national employment in metropolitan areas), other transportation equipment (90 percent), printing and publishing (88 percent), FIRE (88 percent), other transportation services (87 percent), and electrical and other machinery (87 percent). The "least metropolitan" industries are agriculture (29 percent), forestry and fisheries (39 percent), minerals and mining (41 percent), lumber products (45 percent), and textiles (59 percent).

VAPE levels in all of the most metropolitan industries in 1960 were substantially above the national average; together they averaged 52 percent above the national figure (Table 5.2). In contrast four of the five least metropolitan industries were substantially below the national average and together they averaged 22 percent below the national level. Changes in the relative position of the industries' VAPE levels indicate that in the 1940s, increases in VAPE were greater in the least metropolitan industries (averaging 36 percent above the national rate) than in the most metropolitan (averaging 21 percent below the national rate). In the 1950s increases in VAPE were below average in both, but considerably higher in the most metropolitan industries than in the least.

49

TABLE 5.2

Most and Least Metropolitan Industries Compared

	Percent of Nat'l Employment in MLMs[a] 1960	VAPE[b] 1960	Percent of Metropolitan		Change in VAPE[b]		National Employment Growth[b]	
			Exports 1940	(Imports) 1960	1940-50	1950-60	1940-50	1950-60
Most metropolitan								
Motor vehicles	91.4	189	6.0	5.6	125	82	192	−20
Other transportation equipment	90.5	121	2.4	4.8	50	120	215	661
Printing and publishing	87.8	108	2.2	2.3	76	92	132	216
FIRE	87.6	264	5.2	4.9	78	96	115	260
Other transportation (airlines, shipping, taxis, etc.)	86.9	112	2.4	2.6	78	78	222	18
Electrical and other machinery	86.9	119	6.7	10.1	64	87	354	301
Average		152	24.9	30.0	79	92	1,230	1,436
Least metropolitan								
Agriculture	29.0	57	(47.5)	(21.5)	168	69	−67	−248
Forestry and fisheries	39.2	55	(0.6)	(0.5)	150	61	60	−164
Minerals and mining	41.2	124	(5.7)	(3.5)	119	79	5	−192
Lumber products	45.5	76	(4.0)	(4.2)	116	77	100	−67
Textiles	59.0	77	(5.5)	(4.5)	127	70	29	−149
Average		78	63.3	34.2	136	71	127	−820
All industries	75.1	100	100	100	100	100	100	100

aMLM stands for Metropolitan Labor Market.
bPercent of national average.
Source: See Table 3.2.

Differential employment growth in these two types of industries during the 1950s is attributable mainly to differences in the growth of demand. While combined value of output of the most metropolitan industries doubled, combined value of output of the least metropolitan grew only 2.5 percent—not nearly enough to offset their 39 percent gain in VAPE. Employment declined in all five of the least metropolitan industries while it increased in five of the six most metropolitan—all but motor vehicles. In fact, in four of the six, employment expansion was more than twice the national rate.

MAJOR CHANGES IN AGGREGATE METROPOLITAN TRADE

Trends in industry VAPE and consumer expenditure patterns, along with the increased urbanization of the population, have led to significant changes in trade patterns, which are evident in aggregate trade statistics. The three findings, each of which is discussed below, are

(1) that metropolitan trade has declined in importance as a source of employment;

(2) that net metropolitan trade with non-metropolitan areas is declining, and intermetropolitan trade is expanding and becoming relatively more important in the export sectors of metropolitan areas; and

(3) that differences in average VAPE between metropolitan and non-metropolitan areas have narrowed (that is, the employment terms of trade for metropolitan areas has declined, and for non-metropolitan areas it has improved) but are still substantial.

Decline of Importance of Trade in Metropolitan Employment

The metropolitan trade estimates in Table 5.3 reveal immediately the first of these important trends: a decline in the rate of employment expansion in trade activity and a concomitant decline in share of employment accounted for by the metropolitan export sector.

We observe, whereas total metropolitan employment increased by 63 percent during the two decades under study, metropolitan employment in exports increased 44 percent. At the same time, percentage of total employment accounted for by exports declined from 20.9 percent to 18.5 percent.

It should be noted, however, that during the first decade the share of metropolitan employment devoted to export activity increased from 20.9 to 26.6. This was the period during which productivity rose more rapidly in the primary sector, located principally in the non-metropolitan areas, than in the manufacturing and services sectors, located largely in metropolitan places. During the second decade, however, the share of employment accounted for by export activities declined dramatically, from 26.6 percent to 18.8 percent.

51

TABLE 5.3

Metropolitan Trade,
368 Metropolitan Areas Combined

	Employment Equivalents (thousands)			Percent Change		
	1940	1950	1960	1940-50	1950-60	1940-60
Requirements	33,950	43,079	51,683	26.9	20.0	52.0
Employment	30,768	41,120	49,903	30.5	21.4	63.0
Exports	6,417	8,865	9,218	38.1	4.0	44.0
Imports	9,676	10,920	11,107	12.9	1.7	15.0
Percent of employment in exports	20.9	26.6	18.5			

Source: Based on estimates of trade made by using the value added approach described in the text. See Table 3.2.

TABLE 5.4

Metropolitan Trade by Type of Market
(employment equivalents in millions)

	1940	1950	1960
Metropolitan employment	30.76	41.12	49.90
Total metropolitan imports	9.68	10.92	11.11
Imports from non-metropolitan areas	5.01	4.47	3.65
Total metropolitan exports	6.42	8.87	9.22
Exports to non-metropolitan areas	1.75	2.42	1.76
Intermetropolitan trade	4.67	6.45	7.46
Terms of trade: Metropolitan-non-metropolitan places	286	185	207

Source: Based on estimates of trade made by using the value added approach described in text. See Table 3.2.

Declining Importance of Trade with Non-metropolitan Areas
and Increasing Importance of Intermetropolitan Trade

The data in Table 5.4 lead to important observations about the relative importance of trade with non-metropolitan areas and among metropolitan areas. First, trade between metropolitan and non-metropolitan areas has declined significantly. While total metropolitan imports grew over the two decades from 9.68 million to 11.11 million, those metropolitan imports that originated in non-metropolitan areas declined from 5.01 million to 3.65 million. A similar trend is present in metropolitan exports. While total metropolitan exports grew throughout the period from 6.42 million to 9.22 million, the exports to non-metropolitan areas experienced a decade of growth followed by a decade of decline with the net result of little absolute change. However, because total exports were continually rising, the share of exports destined for non-metropolitan areas declined from 27 percent in 1940 to 19 percent in 1960.

This abrupt decline in relative importance of activity between metropolitan areas and the rest of the nation suggests one explanation for the increased difficulty experienced by many non-metropolitan areas in maintaining growth. Metropolitan areas are becoming less dependent on non-metropolitan areas both as a source of imports and as a market for exports. As their traditional trade ties with the rest of the economy are slowly reduced, the more remote non-metropolitan areas are becoming more isolated from and less competitive with the metropolitan sector of the national economy. Unable to increase exports in declining industries, they have declining employment and only minimal export earnings to use for importing goods and services, the prices of which are probably rising. Further, these small communities with lower levels of income generated per employee will be generally less self-sufficient than large metropolitan areas and hence more dependent on imports. Small firms or plants in low-wage industries may be attracted by loose labor market conditions in the declining areas, but these firms do little to enhance the area's growth.

The second observation follows directly from the previous one. While trade between metropolitan and non-metropolitan areas has declined, intermetropolitan trade has expanded. Cities trade primarily with each other. In 1960, 80 percent of metropolitan exports were destined for other metropolitan areas and 67 percent of metropolitan imports originated in other metropolitan areas.

Changes in the Employment Terms of Trade

The ETOT is not only a ratio statistic by which we observe the exchange relationship—the ratio of employment (with accompanying factor inputs) in A to employment (with accompanying factor inputs) in B necessary to affect the exchange of goods and services that has taken place—it is also an index by which to compare certain economic conditions that obtain in different areas, regions, or nations.

It will be recalled that value added represents a flow of income generated, including wages, salaries, depreciation, interest, rent, and profits. As such, it is a statement of dollars available for consumption, investment, and through taxes, for government expenditures. Stated on a per capita or (what is comparable) a per employee basis, it becomes, in effect, a welfare measure: Where VAPE is high, there is a high per capita purchasing power for development of the local service sector, high per capita availability of investment funds for local development, and a high potential tax base for the improvement and enlargement of the public sector.*

Accordingly, a metropolis that specializes in high-VAPE exports and imports low-VAPE industries will have what we shall consider to be an advantageous position in respect to its ETOT. Advantageous in that it retains activities with high-income-generating capacity per worker and imports those activities with low-income-generating effects.

The ETOT may, of course, change over time. Relative VAPE may change by industry. High-VAPE functions may be added or low-VAPE functions may be dropped in the export sector, or high-VAPE functions may be added in the local sector (import substitution) or low-VAPE activities may move out of the metropolis and be replaced by imports (production replacement). As a summary statistic, then, the ETOT indicates the relationship between VAPE in imports and exports and will at a glance tell us how the VAPE structure of imports and exports is changing over time. If, for example, factor incomes increase relatively in the places exporting the output of a particular industry then the employment terms of trade in such places will become more advantageous. More income will be generated and these places will be able to import more (per export worker) from areas where factor costs declined in relative terms. At the same time, rising ETOT reflecting rising VAPE may drive some industries from the metropolis. If these industries are below average VAPE in the area, then the resulting average VAPE will rise further. This was referred to earlier as the upgrading process. The same process is occurring, however, in low-average-VAPE areas such as the non-metropolitan areas.

The findings regarding metropolitan-non-metropolitan terms of trade are indicated in Table 5.4. We see that the terms of trade, which were extremely unfavorable to the non-metropolitan areas in 1940 (286), improved sharply during the 1940s. From 1950 to 1960, however, our estimates indicate a slight deterioration. Thus in 1960 the ratio of employment in non-metropolitan exports to metropolitan places to employment metropolitan exports by non-metropolitan places was still slightly more than two-to-one (207). Thus, we see that non-metropolitan exports not only declined during the two decades but, in spite of some improvement, remained on an unfavorable exchange basis with metropolitan places at the end of the period. It is little wonder that it

---

*It should be noted that where VAPE is high, wages and salaries tend to be high. This is not always the case but is typically true. For the year 1960 the Spearman coefficient of rank correlation between VAPE and average wages for the two-digit manufacturing classifications, was .78.

54

was the metropolitan places that experienced the significant growth and development.

Changes in Industry Trade Patterns

The aggregate trends of increasing self-sufficiency and decreasing trade between metropolitan and non-metropolitan areas and increased significance for intermetropolitan trade do not hold up uniformly for all industrial categories. Table 5.5 reveals that in five of the industry categories, exports increased as a percentage of total metropolitan employment, and in 12 categories the percentage of requirements imported increased. Export employment experienced a relative decline in every manufacturing category but rose notably in public administration, business and repair services, and two business-related transportation categories. The result of these differing industry trade patterns is a significant shift in metropolitan trade activity from goods toward services. Between 1940 and 1960 the percentage of export employment in manufacturing dropped from 53 percent to 49 percent, and the share of export employment in government and services rose from 36 percent to 44 percent.

Metropolitan Trade by Size of Place

Over-all trends in trade differ significantly by size of place, as the data presented in Table 5.6 demonstrate. In the largest places, where constraints on growth are apparently greatest, growth comes not so much from expanding as from upgrading export activity. The high productivity of export activity in larger places is apparent in the ETOT figures.* The employment terms of trade, already found to favor metropolitan over non-metropolitan areas, are most favorable in large places, less favorable in medium-sized places, and unfavorable in small places. In 1940, average VAPE of exports was twice that of imports in large places but less than that of imports in small places. The terms of trade were 198 in large places in 1940, and declined to 149 in 1960; 141 in medium-sized places, dropping to 117 in 1960; and only 95 in small places, falling to 91 in 1960.

Higher VAPE in the export sector contributes to employment gains in the local sector. Thus, even while there was a net decline in export activity (-7 percent) in large metropolitan areas, total employment expanded in the 1950s.

Self-sufficiency increased in all size categories but increased most in the places already most self-sufficient. The share of employment in the export sector declined 3.2 percentage points (from 17.8 to 14.6) in the large category, 2.3 percentage points (from 21.2 to 18.9) in the medium-size class, and only 1.2 percentage points (from 27.1 to 25.9) in the small class. The percent of

---

*These terms of trade statistics are based on trade between each size category of metropolitan place and all other places, both metropolitan and non-metropolitan.

TABLE 5.5

Metropolitan Exports and Imports by Industry

Industry	Exports (thousands) 1940	1950	1960	% Distribution Exports 1940	1950	1960	Exports as % of Total Metro. Employment 1940	1950	1960	Direction of Change (+) (−) 1940-60	Imports as % of Metropolitan Requirements 1940	1950	1960	Direction of Change (+) (−) 1940-60
Primary														
Agriculture	318	264	207	5.0	3.0	2.2	14.8	14.4	16.1	+	71.4	70.4	68.9	−
Forestry, fisheries	16	21	14	0.2	0.2	0.2	40.9	42.0	36.2	−	71.1	69.3	68.0	−
Mining	221	205	142	3.4	2.3	1.5	59.3	58.1	50.3	−	78.3	79.1	74.0	−
Construction	141	472	242	2.2	5.3	2.6	9.2	10.7	8.3	−	11.9	14.3	14.2	+
Manufacturing														
Food, kindred products	200	253	229	3.1	2.9	2.5	21.8	22.0	15.6	−	14.7	17.0	16.6	+
Textile mills	485	501	314	7.6	5.7	3.4	58.2	59.0	53.5	−	60.4	63.3	64.9	+
Apparel manufacturing	326	416	355	5.1	4.7	3.8	45.7	45.8	39.7	−	36.5	39.4	42.9	+
Lumber manufacturing	113	128	109	1.8	1.4	1.2	25.6	24.1	21.5	−	54.2	55.3	54.3	NC
Printing, publishing	140	191	216	2.2	2.2	2.3	24.7	25.0	20.7	−	11.6	12.0	10.9	−
Chemicals, allied	134	193	264	2.1	2.2	2.9	35.4	34.6	35.3	NC	26.8	27.7	31.2	+
Electrical, other machinery	433	770	930	6.7	8.7	10.1	43.3	41.0	33.6	−	30.7	30.2	26.2	−
Motor vehicles, equipment	388	545	512	6.0	6.1	5.6	69.6	66.0	63.9	−	61.4	57.6	57.8	−
Other transportation equipment	156	242	447	2.4	2.7	4.8	53.4	52.6	48.5	−	41.6	40.7	40.4	−
Other miscellaneous manufacturing	1,034	1,243	1,182	16.1	14.0	12.8	32.9	30.3	24.0	−	22.4	20.8	18.2	−

Utilities	55	52	52	0.9	0.6	0.6	12.2	8.4	7.3	—	5.2	6.4	9.8	—
Mainly Business Services														
Railroad, railway express	208	264	193	3.2	3.0	2.1	24.5	25.3	26.0	+	26.0	26.4	28.1	+
Trucking, warehousing	30	55	87	0.5	0.6	0.9	8.1	10.3	11.9	+	11.2	10.5	12.9	+
Other transportation	155	219	240	2.4	2.5	2.6	31.5	28.7	29.8	—	18.7	17.5	22.0	+
Communications	59	96	90	0.9	1.1	1.0	18.0	16.3	12.6	—	10.1	8.8	7.2	—
Wholesale	187	313	295	2.9	3.5	3.2	18.7	18.7	15.3	—	11.9	10.3	9.1	—
FIRE	334	403	455	5.2	4.5	4.9	25.2	23.6	18.5	—	11.5	10.9	8.8	—
Business, repair services	56	79	190	0.9	0.9	2.1	8.6	8.0	13.8	+	9.4	9.5	9.3	NC
Mainly Consumer Services														
Food, dairy stores	69	61	40	1.1	0.7	0.4	6.0	4.7	3.1	—	4.0	5.5	7.5	+
Eating, drinking places	112	130	82	1.7	1.5	0.9	12.5	9.8	5.7	—	8.1	7.6	8.1	NC
Other retail	210	295	242	3.3	3.3	2.6	7.2	7.3	5.0	—	4.9	5.7	8.0	+
Hotel, other personal services	183	182	161	2.9	2.1	1.7	13.5	12.3	10.3	—	9.2	9.2	10.8	+
Entertainment, recreation	68	72	78	1.1	0.8	0.8	20.7	17.7	17.8	—	13.5	11.7	12.2	—
Medical, other professions	182	358	439	2.8	4.0	4.8	7.3	9.7	7.2	NC	8.8	8.4	7.8	—
Government														
Public administration	213	464	562	3.3	5.2	6.1	18.1	22.5	20.7	+	14.6	16.6	17.7	+
Armed forces	189	580	851	2.9	6.5	9.2	68.5	65.1	59.3	—	62.7	60.2	58.6	—
All Industries	6,417	8,865	9,218	100.0	100.0	100.0	20.9	21.6	18.5	—	28.5	25.3	21.5	—

Source: Based on estimates of trade made by using the value added approach described in the text. See Table 3.2.

57

TABLE 5.6

Metropolitan Trade by Size of Place
(employment equivalents, thousands)

	Employment	Exports	Imports	ETOT*	Exports as Percent of Employment
Total: 368 places					
1940	30,768	6,417	9,676	151	20.9
1950	41,120	8,865	10,920	123	21.6
1960	49,903	9,218	11,107	120	18.5
Large places: 13 (over 1.6 million)					
1940	12,818	2,286	4,524	198	17.8
1950	16,584	3,033	4,522	149	18.3
1960	19,347	2,825	4,215	149	14.6
Medium places: 114 (200,001 to 1,600,000)					
1940	12,510	2,654	3,750	141	21.2
1950	17,241	3,826	4,536	119	22.2
1960	21,803	4,125	4,830	117	18.9
Small places: 241 (25,001 to 200,000)					
1940	5,443	1,477	1,402	95	27.1
1950	7,295	2,006	1,862	93	27.5
1960	8,753	2,268	2,062	91	25.9

*These terms of trade statistics are based on trade between each size category of metropolitan place and all other places, both metropolitan and non-metropolitan.

Source: Based on estimates of trade made by using the value added approach described in the text. See Table 3.2.

requirements imported also declined in all categories (not shown in Table 5.6), but the same pattern prevailed—a decline of 9.8, 5.8, and 2.1 percentage points in the large, medium, and small categories, respectively.

In sum, exports from large places tend to be in high-VAPE industries and imports to them tend to be in low-VAPE industries. As size of place decreases, average VAPE in industries exported tends to decline and average VAPE in industries imported tends to increase. Such trade patterns, or spatial ordering of industries by size of place, explain why average productivity (VAPE) and self-sufficiency tend to increase with size of metropolis.

Metropolitan Trade by Type of Place

Trade patterns also differ among different types of places.* This is evident in the following figures:

Type of Place	Share of Employment In Exports
Nodal	14.9
Manufacturing	19.7
Armed forces	32.9
Medical-educational	29.5
Resort	30.3
Mixed	18.4
Mixed with nodal characteristics	15.7

Clearly, export activity accounts for a smaller share of employment in places where the export sector is diversified (nodal type, mixed type with nodal characteristics, and all mixed-type places) than in places in which the export sector is specialized (manufacturing, medical-educational services, resort activities, and armed forces).

It is interesting that employment terms of trade also vary widely. They are most favorable in manufacturing and nodal places (139 and 135, respectively). They are most unfavorable in places specialized in the armed forces (74), medical-educational services (78), and resort activities (81)—specialized chiefly, then, in low-VAPE industries, which tend, moreover, to be located in small or medium-sized places. Indeed, it is expected that in each type of place, size affects the percent of employment and VAPE in exports and the ETOT.

In respect to the composition of export trade by type of place, the several trade patterns are what one would expect on the basis of the classifications used (Table 5.7). Diversified services dominate exports in nodal-type places. In manufacturing-type places, exports are limited almost entirely to manufacturing-type activities, which account for 91.8 percent of total exports. Medical-educational centers were less specialized; only 55.5 percent of exports were in medical, educational, and other professional services; the remaining exports were evenly distributed among goods and services. Manufacturing exports were,

---

*Classification of places by (function) type is based on the industrial composition of employment in 1960. Since the classification of a place may change over time, the analysis of trade by type of place is limited to the year for which places were classified, 1960. See Thomas M. Stanback and Richard V. Knight, *The Metropolitan Economy: The Process of Employment Expansion* (New York: Columbia University Press, 1970), p. 6.

TABLE 5.7

Industrial Composition of Employment in Exports by Type of Place, 1960*
(percent distribution)

Industry	Nodal	Mfg.	Armed Forces	Medical-Educat.	Resort	Mixed	Mixed in Nodal Char.
Primary	2.9	1.1	1.9	4.3	6.6	20.7	6.2
Agriculture	1.2	0.4	1.2	4.0	6.3	14.1	3.0
Forestry, fisheries	0.1	0.1	0.3	0.2	0.3	0.3	0.3
Mining	1.6	0.6	0.4	0.1		6.3	2.9
Construction	3.0	0.2	2.8	4.3	17.3	3.5	5.4
Manufacturing	37.0	91.8	10.1	14.5	2.5	39.6	45.1
Food, kindred products	2.6	2.2	0.9	1.9		5.7	3.5
Textile mills	0.6	8.5	2.2	1.4		1.6	1.6
Apparel manufacturing	6.4	3.9	0.1	0.2	1.8	1.3	3.7
Lumber manufacturing	0.5	1.6	0.5	0.6	0.6	1.7	3.4
Printing, publishing	4.5	1.4	0.9	0.7	0.1	0.4	2.2
Chemicals, allied	1.8	4.2	0.5	0.2		4.9	5.9
Electrical, other machinery	9.0	18.4		3.1		3.9	11.4
Motor vehicles, equipment	0.4	16.8		1.9		2.5	1.0
Other transportation equipment	7.1	3.3	4.6	0.1		7.8	1.6
Other miscellaneous manufacturing	4.1	31.5	0.4	4.4		9.8	10.8
Utilities	0.6	0.2	0.3	0.3	1.3	1.4	1.2
Mainly Business Services	37.8	3.9	4.3	2.1	13.6	11.0	11.0
Railroad, railway express	2.4	1.6	0.8	0.2	0.3	5.3	2.5
Trucking, warehousing	1.5	0.9	0.1			0.9	0.9
Other transportation	6.4	0.2	1.2		1.2	1.5	0.6
Communications	2.2	0.1	0.2	0.5	1.4	0.4	1.0
Wholesale	8.1	0.2	0.6		0.5	1.9	1.8
FIRE	12.2	0.8	0.8	1.1	6.1	0.6	2.6
Business, repair services	5.0	0.1	0.6	0.3	4.1	0.4	1.6
Mainly Consumer Services	14.5	1.7	7.0	64.5	53.8	11.6	18.0
Food, dairy stores	0.5	0.3	0.2	0.4	1.7	1.0	0.7
Eating, drinking places	1.3	0.1	0.5	1.2	7.5	1.1	1.2
Other retail	4.0	0.3	1.5	3.6	10.5	4.2	4.3
Hotel, other personal services	2.3	0.1	1.4	3.6	23.6	1.2	2.1
Entertainment, recreation	1.8		0.2	0.2	9.0	0.3	0.3
Medical, other professions	4.6	0.9	3.2	55.5	1.5	3.8	9.4
Government	4.2	1.0	73.6	9.8	5.0	12.3	13.0
Public administration	2.3	0.7	24.6	5.0	2.0	7.5	7.1
Armed forces	1.9	0.3	49.0	4.8	3.0	4.8	5.9
All Industries	100.0	100.0	100.0	100.0	100.0	100.0	100.0

*The Starback-Knight classification of MLMs.

Source: Based on trade estimates made by using the value added approach described in the text. See Table 3.2.

however, almost nonexistent in resort centers. Over half of the exports from these places were in the recreation and entertainment, hotels and other personal services, and retailing categories. The tendency for resort cities to specialize also in producer services is clear; business and repair services accounted for almost as large a share of exports from resort-type places (4.1 percent) as from nodal-type places (5.0 percent); FIRE accounted for 6.1 percent of exports. Mixed-type places represent a combination of agricultural centers, mining centers, railroad junctures, and combinations of these and manufacturing activities.

Aggregate Trade and Employment Expansion

Although trade patterns vary significantly by type of place and size of place, it is useful to examine the relationship between changes in metropolitan trade and employment expansion. The relative importance of changes in trade may best be understood by identifying sources of job increases and decreases, as was done for Huntsville, Alabama. Table 5.8 summarizes the employment effects of changes in trade activity for all metropolitan places.

TABLE 5.8

Aggregate Job-Increase-Job-Decrease Analysis
(employment equivalents, thousands)

	1940-50		1950-60	
	Number	Percent	Number	Percent
Job increases				
Increased exports	3,035	26.2	2,152	19.3
Decreased imports	324	2.8	569	5.1
(Import substitution)	(707)	(6.1)	(1,003)	(9.0)
Changes in local demand	8,224	71.0	8,429	75.6
Total	11,583	100.0	11,150	100.0
Job decreases				
Decreased exports	260	21.9	1,040	43.8
Increased imports	155	13.0	290	12.2
Changes in local demand	755	65.1	1,045	44.0
Total	1,170	100.0	2,375	100.0
Net Change	10,413		8,775	

Source: Based on trade estimates made by using the value added approach described in the text. See Table 3.2.

61

The first observation is that increases in local demand accounted for a very large share of job increases in both decades and was even more important in the second decade (75.6 percent) than in the first (71 percent). This reflects the general increase in the size of MTMs noted in Chapter 4 as well as the declining importance of export activity.

The aggregate figures also support the observation that metropolitan areas are becoming more self-sufficient. This is clearly indicated by the fact that increased exports played a smaller role in job creation in the second decade, while decreased exports played a larger role in job declines.* The trend toward self-sufficiency is also evident in the expanding role of decreased imports in job creation. If the relative measure of import declines—import substitution—is used, we find even more evidence of growing self-sufficiency; import substitution accounted for 6 percent of the job increases in the first decade and 9 percent in the second decade.

Table 5.9 provides industry breakdowns for the job-creation component of the aggregate analysis; included are figures for the relative measure referred to as import substitution. The table reveals that the various industrial sectors contributed in quite different degrees to the several categories of job creation. Manufacturing accounted for 34.7 percent of all job increases, only 29.5 percent of the local demand increases, 47.1 percent of the export increases, and 63.4 percent of the import substitution. Examination of the detailed industry classifications within manufacturing reveals that gains attributable to local demand were fairly evenly distributed, but export increases were concentrated to a significant extent in electrical and other machinery and other transportation equipment.

Business services accounted for 15.7 percent of all increases and 10.9 percent of import declines. A substantial portion of the business service gains, and particularly those in local demand, are in the FIRE classification. This is evidence of the proliferation of banking, insurance, real estate, and brokerage services at the local level that has accompanied the rise of affluence in America. The fact that the FIRE and business and repair services classifications together account for most of the gains in business services due to export increases points to a rising specialization of some metropolitan centers in the rendering of these business services.

The most striking observation from Table 5.8 concerns the consumer services category. It accounted for more than one-third of all job increases and 40 percent of the job gains attributable to local demand. Two classifications dominated this category—medical-educational services and retailing (21-23). Job increases in the first represent the rising tide of demand that accompanied the new concern for delivery of health services and the urgent need to educate the "baby-boom" generation—a demand underwritten by rapidly rising per capita income. Job increases in the second reflect the growth and rising affluence of the American economy.

_____

*It is interesting to note also that there was increasing industrial transition in the export sector during the 1950s; three-fifths of the job increases in export activity were offset by declining exports in other industries in the same metropolis, compared to one-fifth in the 1940s.

TABLE 5.9

Analysis of Job Increases, 1950-60
(percent distribution)

Industry	Code	Total	Local Demand	Export Increase	Import Increase	Import Substitution[b]
Primary		0.7	0.2	1.8	3.5	1.9
Agriculture	1	0.2	0.1	0.4	0.5	0.3
Forestry, fisheries	2	a	a	0.1	0.3	0.2
Mining	3	0.5	0.1	1.3	2.7	1.4
Construction	4	3.3	3.4	2.9	4.2	3.6
Manufacturing		34.7	29.5	47.1	63.7	63.4
Food, kindred products	5	2.8	3.3	1.6	2.3	3.1
Textile mills	6	0.2	a	0.5	1.3	0.8
Apparel manufacturing	7	0.7	0.5	1.3	1.8	1.7
Lumber manufacturing	8	5.5	3.2	7.7	26.2	22.1
Printing, publishing	9	2.4	2.7	1.7	1.8	2.1
Chemicals, allied	10	1.9	1.4	3.9	1.2	1.4
Electrical, other machinery	11	8.4	7.7	11.5	8.1	9.8
Motor vehicles, equipment	12	0.9	0.2	3.2	2.5	1.7
Other transportation equipment	13	4.4	2.7	11.4	2.4	3.3
Other miscellaneous manufacturing	14	7.5	7.8	4.3	16.1	17.4
Utilities	19	0.9	1.0	0.7	0.6	0.4
Mainly Business Services		15.7	17.2	14.7	10.9	10.0
Railroad, railway express	15	a	a	—	a	a
Trucking, warehousing	16	1.7	1.9	1.6	1.3	1.1
Other transportation	17	0.7	0.5	1.7	0.4	0.4
Communications	18	1.1	1.2	0.7	1.6	1.0
Wholesale	20	2.2	2.3	1.8	3.4	2.6
FIRE	24	6.5	8.1	3.4	1.4	3.1
Business, repair services	27	3.5	3.2	5.5	2.8	1.8
Mainly Consumer Services		33.6	40.0	11.2	12.0	14.4
Food, dairy stores	21	0.7	0.8	0.3	1.0	0.6
Eating, drinking places	22	1.1	1.2	0.4	1.9	1.1
Other retail	23	6.5	8.1	2.0	3.6	3.1
Hotel, other personal services	25	1.1	8.2	1.5	0.7	0.5
Private households	26	1.8	—	—	—	—
Entertainment, recreation	28	0.4	0.3	0.5	0.6	0.3
Medical, other professions	29	22.0	28.4	6.5	4.2	8.9
Government		11.0	8.8	21.6	5.4	6.5
Public administration	30	5.6	5.9	6.1	2.6	2.8
Armed forces	31	5.4	2.9	15.5	2.8	3.7
Total		100.0	100.0	100.0	100.0	100.0
Number		11,150,000 (100%)	8,429,400 (75.6%)	2,151,950 (19.3%)	568,650 (5.1%)	1,003,500 (9.0%)

aDenotes less than 0.1 percent.

bIncludes import decreases and a portion of local demand.

Source: Based on trade estimates made by using the value added approach described in the text. See Table 3.2.

Job decreases were much smaller than job increases (see Table 5.8) and do not require detailed examination. An industrial breakdown (not shown) reveals that over half (55.4 percent) the decreases were in the primary sector. In large part this is because county building blocks were used to construct the SMSAs that comprise most of the metropolitan economies. In the rural fringes of these SMSAs, job decreases in agriculture were of considerable importance. Within the manufacturing sector, which accounted for one-fifth (20.3 percent) of the job decreases, job destruction was concentrated in textile mill products, lumber manufacturing, and motor vehicles. Many of the job decreases in textiles and motor vehicles represent relocations of production: in textiles from metro-politan areas to non-metropolitan areas; in motor vehicles from one metro-politan area to another. Most of the remaining job decreases were in business services (13.3 percent) and were concentrated in the railroad and railway express categories. Consumer services and government accounted for very few job declines.

SUMMARY

In this chapter, changes in national employment patterns were analyzed, and the trends were related to aggregate trade patterns. The trade patterns were then analyzed in terms of metropolitan-to-non-metropolitan trade, trade by size of place, and trade by type of place. Finally, aggregate trade changes were related to the sources of metropolitan growth.

It was found that while total employment in trade expanded in both decades of the period 1940 to 1960, the growth was not evenly distributed among all industries. Growth varied both because of changes in demand and changes in VAPE. For the two decades as a whole, changes in VAPE offset changes in demand in industries concentrated in non-metropolitan areas; consequently, employment in these areas grew at a much slower rate than in metropolitan areas.

Aggregate trade statistics pointed to an increasing self-sufficiency of metropolitan areas during the most recent decade. Between 1950 and 1960, employment in the local sector grew from 74.1 percent to 81 percent of total metropolitan employment, and the proportion of requirements imported by cities dropped from 25.3 percent to 21.5 percent. The terms of trade continued to favor metropolitan over non-metropolitan areas throughout the period, but the relative advantage declined as indicated in the ETOT ratio of 207 in 1960 versus 286 in 1940. Trade between metropolitan areas became more important over the period, while trade between metropolis and hinterland declined in significance. Between 1940 and 1960, the share of metropolitan exports that were destined for non-metropolitan areas declined from 27 percent to 19 percent, and the share of exports traded between metropolitan areas grew from 73 percent to 81 percent.

Aggregate trends did not apply uniformly to all sectors of the economy. Despite the general trend toward greater self-sufficiency, exports experienced a relative increase in five industry categories, four of which were in the service sector. The result is a shift toward services in trade activity; services accounted for 44 percent of all employment in the export sector in 1960 compared to 36 percent in 1940.

The trend toward increased self-sufficiency was present in all cities, but was most pronounced in the larger areas. The share of employment in the local sector grew from 82.2 percent to 85.4 percent in large cities, from 78.8 percent to 81.1 percent in medium-sized cities, and from 72.9 percent to 74.1 percent in small cities. The greater self-sufficiency in larger places can be attributed to the higher level of VAPE in their export sectors. By type of place, the local sector (and, hence, self-sufficiency) was greatest in places with a diversified export sector (nodal and mixed with nodal characteristics) and smallest in specialized places (armed forces and resort).

A job-increase-job-decrease analysis based on the components of trade for the two decades 1940-50 and 1950-60 indicated that expansion in production for local demand was the most significant source of growth in both periods. Expanded export activity accounted for only 26 percent and 19 percent of the job increases in the respective decades. Job decreases are far less numerous than job increases in metropolitan places, but decreases due to declining export activity grew sharply from 22 percent of all decreases in the first decade to 44 percent in the second.

6

REGIONAL TRADE
PATTERNS

Regional trade patterns reflect the spatial organization of the national economy—that is, the dominant functions of metropolitan and non-metropolitan areas in each region and the scope of their markets. It is known that there is considerable trade within and among regions, but the extent of trade in terms of the employment it represents in each industry in each region has never been quantified. An attempt is made here to estimate, for each industrial category, interregional trade and intraregional trade. Intraregional trade is then disaggregated into intermetropolitan trade and trade between metropolitan and non-metropolitan areas within a region.

RELATIVE IMPORTANCE OF INTER- AND INTRA-REGIONAL TRADE

Table 6.1 presents estimates of total metropolitan trade (exports or imports) for each industry, total trade as a percent of metropolitan requirements, the share of each industry's metropolitan exports (imports) that are destined for (originate in) another region, and the share of exports (imports) that are destined for (originate in) the same region.*

Throughout this analysis of regional trade patterns, the reader should bear in mind that trade is only a fraction of requirements in each industry and that in most industries the fraction is declining. In all industries combined metropolitan areas imported only 21.5 percent of their requirements, and, as

---

*Since the U.S. economy is assumed to be a closed economy, interregional exports and interregional imports in all regions combined are equal; what is imported by one region must be exported by another. Similarly, total intraregional imports will equal total intraregional exports.

noted earlier (See Table 5.3), trade activity accounted for only 18.5 percent of total metropolitan employment.

Clearly, interregional trade dominates intraregional trade. In 23 of the 30 industry categories the interregional component is the larger share, and in no industry is it less than 39.8 percent of total metropolitan trade in that industry. The industries in which interregional trade is relatively most important are textiles (95.6 percent), apparel (89.9), motor vehicles (88.9), hotels (86.0), and other retail stores (84.0). Those in which interregional trade is least important are food and kindred (39.8), railroads (40.0), wholesaling (40.0), FIRE (40.9), medical and other professional (46.0), and public administration (47.0).

Interregional Trade

Detailed estimates of the regional origins of the interregional component of metropolitan trade are presented in Table 6.2.* Figures are presented for 1940, 1950, and 1960, so that trends in interregional trade patterns can be observed.

Over four-fifths of the interregional trade in agriculture originated in the Southeast and Plains regions. Between 1940 and 1960 the Southeast's share of interregional trade in agriculture declined from 62 to 43 percent. Exports in mining increased in the Southwest from 22 to 43 percent. Exports in forestry and fisheries and lumber manufacturing originated primarily in the Southeast and West Coast regions.

Interregional export activity in the food and kindred products industries, concentrated almost exclusively in the Plains region in 1960, has been almost entirely phased out in the Great Lakes, from which the stockyards, for example, have moved to centers west, such as Omaha.

Exports of textile mill products continued to shift from New England to the Southeast, which accounted for 86 percent of interregional trade in textiles in 1960. Apparel exports from the Southeast showed up for the first time in 1960; before that, the Middle Atlantic region dominated this trade activity.

The Great Lakes region dominates interregional exports in three important manufacturing categories: motor vehicles (in which it supplies 100 percent of interregional exports), electrical and other machinery (67 percent), and other and miscellaneous manufacturing (46 percent). Other transportation equipment manufacturing is another industry that is regionally concentrated. Approximately 80 percent of employment attributable to interregional exports in this industry is located in the West Coast region. The other 20 percent is in New England. The Middle Atlantic region, an exporter in 1950, had become a net importer by 1960.

In 1940, interregional exports in utilities were concentrated primarily (69 percent) in the Middle Atlantic region. By 1960, the region had become a net

---

*Interregional trade is measured the same way as metropolitan trade (Chapter 2). The region that includes all metropolitan and non-metropolitan areas is taken as the basic unit of analysis. Exports and imports are estimated for each region using the value added approach.

TABLE 6.1

Regional Trade Patterns by Industry, 1960
(employment equivalents, thousands)

Industry	Metropolitan Requirements	Total Metropolitan Trade Exports (Imports)	Total Metropolitan Trade as Percent of Requirements	Interregional Trade*	Intraregional Trade*	Interregional Trade as Percent of Total Trade
Primary						
Agriculture	3,467	(2,387)	68.8	1,286	1,101	53.9
Forestry, fisheries	76	(51)	67.1	35	16	68.6
Mining	533	(394)	78.9	242	152	61.4
Construction	3,108	(442)	14.2	353	89	79.9
Manufacturing						
Food, kindred products	1,484	(246)	16.6	98	148	39.8
Textile mills	777	(504)	64.9	482	22	95.6
Apparel manufacturing	944	(405)	42.9	364	49	89.9
Lumber manufacturing	869	(472)	54.3	308	164	65.2
Printing, publishing	929	216	23.3	131	85	60.4
Chemicals, allied	704	264	37.5	124	140	75.6
Electrical, other machinery	2,488	930	37.4	733	197	78.8
Motor vehicles, equipment	686	512	74.6	455	57	88.9
Other transportation equipment	796	447	56.2	241	206	53.9

Other miscellaneous manufacturing	4,585	1,182	25.8	915	267	77.4
Utilities	732	(72)	9.8	43	29	59.7
Mainly Business Services						
Railroad, railway express	767	(215)	28.0	86	129	40.0
Trucking, warehousing	742	(96)	12.9	52	56	54.2
Other transportation	723	240	33.2	125	115	52.1
Communications	668	90	13.5	44	46	48.9
Wholesale	1,802	295	16.4	118	131	40.0
FIRE	2,195	455	20.7	186	26.9	40.9
Business, repair services	1,312	190	14.5	107	83	56.3
Mainly Consumer Services						
Food, dairy stores	1,376	(103)	7.5	80	43	58.1
Eating, drinking places	1,467	(119)	8.1	73	46	61.3
Other retail	4,958	(395)	8.0	332	63	84.0
Hotel, other personal services	1,581	(171)	10.8	147	24	86.0
Entertainment, recreation	410	78	19.0	50	28	64.1
Medical, other professions	6,172	(482)	7.8	222	276	46.0
Government						
Public administration	2,608	562	21.5	264	298	47.0
Armed forces	1,412	851	60.3	582	285	68.4

*Exports equal imports.

Source: Based on the trade estimates made by using the value added approach described in the text. See Table 3.2.

TABLE 6.2

Regional Origin of Interregional Trade by Industry
(employment, thousands)

Industry	New England 1940	1950	1960	Middle Atlantic 1940	1950	1960	Great Lakes 1940	1950	1960	Plains 1940	1950	1960
Primary												
Agriculture										693	735	555
Forestry, fisheries	3	6	3									
Mining												
Construction											10	1
Manufacturing												
Food, kindred products							28	23	3	50	72	82
Textile mills	175	180	66									
Apparel manufacturing	8	6	9	267	356	296						
Lumber manufacturing												
Printing, publishing		1	4	40	65	83	23	27	40	1		4
Chemicals, allied				49	67	78						
Electrical, other machinery	65	105	138	25	82	105	227	438	490			
Motor vehicles, equipment							339	487	455			
Other transportation equipment	18	15	50	39	18							
Other miscellaneous manufacturing	215	220	211	247	343	288	301	401	416			
Utilities				24	1						1	5
Mainly Business Services												
Railroad, railway express							6	4	20	41	58	48
Trucking, warehousing								9	17	17	22	20
Other transportation				49	72	77						
Communications	1			9	22	19				4	1	2
Wholesale					20	15				47	40	31
FIRE	2	12	10	129	134	125						
Business, repair services						32				15	21	
Mainly Consumer Services												
Food, dairy stores	1			31	18							
Eating, drinking places										11	13	17
Other retail										50	66	79
Hotel, other personal services										3		
Entertainment, recreation						2						
Medical, other professions	17	24	26	2	9					59	48	87
Goverment												
Public administration				63	73	78				6		
Armed forces												

	Southeast			Southwest			Rocky Mountain			Far West			Nation		
	1940	1950	1960	1940	1950	1960	1940	1950	1960	1940	1950	1960	1940	1950	1960
	1,958	1,346	555	438	218	108	83	90	68				3,172	2,389	1,286
	35	31	22						2	6	10	7	44	47	34
	118	156	83	64	90	126	35	27	33				217	273	242
	49	98	193	33	111	102	6	23	21	43	83	28	131	325	345
									1	13	15		91	110	86
	306	373	416										481	553	482
			59										275	362	364
	212	277	223							75	97	85	287	374	308
										1			65	93	131
	29	28	46										78	95	124
													317	625	733
													335	487	455
										40	88	191	97	121	241
													763	964	915
			11		14	23	1	3	4	10	12		35	31	43
	18	4					19	26	18				84	92	96
				8	7	9	1	4	6	1			27	42	52
			18	3	4	4				20	19	18	72	95	117
						5	2	3	3	9	20	20	25	41	44
				22	18	35	5	4	6	44	50	31	118	132	118
						3				32	47	48	163	193	186
				12	13	20	5	7	1	21	30	54	53	71	107
		22	45	10	10	15				4			40	50	60
				16	26	18	3	9	12	33	44	25	63	92	72
		8	138	50	78	93	13	17	21	43	65	1	156	234	332
	11	36	75	29	37	42	6	7	10	33	31	18	82	111	145
				1	1		1	2	1	39	40	46	41	43	49
				18	19	20	15	22	34	24	72	55	135	194	222
			29		19	37	10	20	30	16	79	70	95	191	246
	21	134	227	15	67	110	3	5	5	40	138	166	79	344	508

Source: Based on trade estimates made by using the value added approach described in the text. See Table 3.2.

importer, and the Southeast and Southwest regions, net importers in 1940, accounted for 80 percent of export activity in the industry. Such shifts in the location of industrial activity in primary and manufacturing activities suggest some of the dynamics of past economic development and demonstrate how trade activity data may serve to identify them.

A relatively clear distinction can be drawn between interregional exports east of the Mississippi and interregional exports west of the Mississippi. Exports in manufacturing industries, except in other transportation equipment, originate to the east, and exports of resource activities and services, except those services exported from national centers, such as New York, Washington, D.C., and Boston, originate to the west. In the future, however, the dichotomy between regions specialized in manufacturing and those specialized in nonmanufacturing is almost certain to weaken. National parameters, factors affecting the location of industries, and interindustry linkages will change as metropolitan and regional economies develop. The relative importance of employment in manufacturing will continue to decline, while that in service industries continues to increase. Furthermore, the lower-productivity and manufacturing industries are most likely to continue to relocate in smaller labor markets in the less developed regions.

It is also conceivable that the increasing concern with environmental factors will be acute in regions where manufacturing is presently concentrated and that pollution controls will become a serious constraint on further growth. Internalizing environmental pollution cost will naturally affect total operating costs. Just as the "nuisance" or "noxious" industries, such as glue factories, slaughterhouses, and chemical plants, have dispersed away from major urban areas, so the "polluting" industries may relocate in (disperse to) regions whose pollution controls are less restrictive or whose ecological systems can accommodate the pollution for a longer period. On the other hand, it is quite possible that the less urbanized areas will become increasingly cautious in encouraging economic growth and show more discretion in attracting industries.

Intraregional Trade

The intraregional component of total metropolitan trade is analyzed in Table 6.3. It should be kept in mind throughout the interpretation of Table 6.3 that in most cases intraregional trade is only a small portion of total regional trade. The data for total intraregional trade are broken down into trade between cities within the region and trade between metropolitan areas and non-metropolitan areas (hinterland) within the region.*

---

*Intraregional trade in a given industry among metropolitan areas and between metropolitan areas and non-metropolitan areas may be computed as follows:

(1) Intraregional trade among metropolitan areas is estimated by separately summing exports and imports for all metropolitan areas in the region. The smaller sum will represent intraregional trade between metropolitan areas (that is, we assume that metropolitan areas trade first with other metropolitan areas in the same region).

(2) Trade between metropolitan and non-metropolitan areas is estimated as the difference between the net regional metropolitan trade balance (that is, the sum of metropolitan exports minus the sum of metropolitan imports) and net interregional trade.

TABLE 6.3

Intraregional Trade

Industry	Total Intraregional Trade (thousands)	Trade Between Cities (percent)	Trade Between City and Hinterland (percent)
Primary			
Agriculture	1,101	24.5	75.5
Forestry, fisheries	16	81.3	18.7
Mining	152	52.0	48.0
Construction	89	67.4	32.6
Manufacturing			
Food, kindred products	148	90.5	9.5
Textile mills	22	100.0	0.0
Apparel manufacturing	49	8.2	91.8
Lumber manufacturing	164	63.4	36.6
Printing, publishing	85	62.4	37.6
Chemicals, allied	140	96.4	3.6
Electrical, other machinery	197	100.0	0.0
Motor vehicles, equipment	57	100.0	0.0
Other transportation equipment	206	87.0	13.0
Other miscellaneous manufacturing	267	100.0	0.0
Utilities	20	79.3	20.7
Mainly Business Services			
Railroad, railway express	129	86.0	14.0
Trucking, warehousing	56	82.1	17.9
Other transportation	115	72.2	27.8
Communications	46	67.4	32.6
Wholesale	131	43.5	56.5
FIRE	169	82.8	17.8
Business, repair services	83	84.3	15.7
Mainly Consumer Services			
Food, dairy stores	43	55.8	44.2
Eating, drinking places	46	60.9	39.1
Other retail	63	79.4	20.6
Hotel, other personal services	24	87.5	12.5
Entertainment, recreation	28	75.0	25.0
Medical, other professions	276	93.5	6.5
Government			
Public administration	298	80.9	19.1
Armed forces	285	96.1	3.9

Source: Based on trade estimates made by using the value added approach described in the text. See Table 3.2.

The figures indicate that trade between metropolitan areas dominates intraregional trade. In only three industries (agriculture, apparel, and wholesaling) was trade between metropolitan areas less than half of intraregional trade. This supports the earlier finding that aggregate metropolitan trade was increasingly between cities and that trade between metropolitan and non-metropolitan areas was experiencing a relative decline. The finding also emphasizes the importance of regional systems or hierarchies of cities. Within a region, there are cities of varying sizes, and the functions of each vary. Specialized goods produced in the larger cities (regional centers) are traded for goods or services produced in smaller cities within the region. However, it should be noted that in agriculture, which is the single industry that accounts for the largest share of intraregional trade, trade is primarily between city and hinterland.

So far, our analysis has pointed to several dimensions of regional trade. First, there is the extent to which regions trade with each other (interregional trade) and, second, the degree to which this interregional trade is concentrated in one or more regions. Third, there is the degree to which trade is intraregional and to which intraregional trade is distributed between intercity and hinterland-city trade. For any single industry these dimensions can be combined to yield differing regional trade patterns.

ANALYSIS OF THREE INDUSTRIES

Table 6.4 presents data on the multidimensional regional trade patterns for three industries that are fairly representative configurations. For each region, figures are provided showing the exports (imports) that originate in (are destined for) the metropolitan areas of the region, the exports (imports) that originate in (are destined for) the hinterland areas of the region, and the exports (imports) that are destined for (originate in) other regions. For any one region, the figures for hinterland and metropolitan trade will add algebraically to yield interregional exports (imports). Total interregional exports will equal total interregional imports.

Lumber and wood products manufacturing represents a geographically dispersed non-metropolitan type of industry. Regional hinterland areas are exporters of this activity in all regions except the Plains; metropolitan areas are importers in all regions including the Southeast and Far West, which export lumber manufacturing to the other regions as a result of the substantial production in their hinterlands. Interregional trade in lumber manufacturing, originating primarily in non-metropolitan areas, accounted for 308,000 jobs in 1960.

Motor vehicle manufacturing represents a metropolitan industry concentrated in the Great Lakes region. Even non-metropolitan areas in the Great Lakes region are exporters of the industry, but they account for only 17,000 of the 455,000 jobs represented by interregional exports. All other regions are importers of this industry.

74

TABLE 6.4

Inter- and Intraregional Dimensions of Trade
in Three Selected Industries, 1960
(exports = +, imports = −)
(employment, thousands)

Industry	New England	Middle Atlan- tic	Great Lakes	Plains	South- east	South- west	Rocky Mtns.	Far West	Pacific*
Lumber Manufacturing									
Metropolitan areas	−33	−143	−94	−34	−5	−36	−11	−4	−3
Hinterland	16	5	19	−15	228	2	9	89	0
Interregional	−17	−138	−75	−49	223	−34	−2	85	−3
Motor Vehicles									
Metropolitan areas	−43	−87	438	−11	−71	−38	−11	−58	−3
Hinterland	−6	−10	17	−26	−56	−17	−7	−8	−1
Interregional	−49	−97	455	−37	−127	−55	−18	−66	−4
FIRE									
Metropolitan areas	17	149	−53	27	33	24	7	58	−1
Hinterland	−7	−24	−51	−31	−96	−21	−8	−10	−2
Interregional	10	125	−104	−4	−63	3	−1	48	−3

*Alaska and Hawaii.

Source: Based on trade estimates made by using the value added approach described in the text. See Table 3.2.

The extent of motor vehicle imports in the Southwest raises interesting questions about regional thresholds, interindustry linkages, and regional growth. Imports of motor vehicles into the Southeast represent 127,000 jobs and 80 percent of the region's requirements; this would certainly appear to represent a market sufficient to support a regional industry. At what point, we may ask, will the motor vehicle industry move from regional assembly plants to a second major vertically integrated complex? It is interesting to speculate on the impact that such a development would have on the regions affected. It could represent a shift of 127,000 workers, who with their families would constitute nearly half a million people, to the Southeast region. In addition, an equal number of workers probably would be needed in the satellite industries and related activities that would follow. Moreover, the expansion of jobs in the local sector as a result of the multiplier effect would outnumber workers in motor vehicles by approximately 6 to 1. In short, labor market conditions in the two regions affected would be substantially changed; the greatly accel- erated development of the Southeast region would cause the shift of approximately 1 million to 1.5 million workers or 2.5 million to 4 million people. The regional trade multiplier would increase, and since VAPE in the region would rise, the region's terms of trade would improve.

Finance, insurance, and real estate represents a third type of regional trade pattern, one in which metropolitan areas are the major exporters and interregional exports are limited primarily to two regions. Nationally, intraregional trade accounts for 59 percent of trade activity in FIRE (See Table 6.1), and of this intraregional trade, less than 20 percent is attributable to metropolitan exports to regional hinterlands (See Table 6.3). Only in the Great Lakes and Pacific regions are metropolitan areas importers of these services. The substantial imports in the Great Lakes suggests that perhaps durable-goods manufacturing such as motor vehicles and the rendering of business services by independent firms such as FIRE are not fully compatible. Business services are probably internalized within the larger firms and are not available to smaller firms, which must import them. The Great Lakes is deficient in business service activities, just as the Southeast is deficient in consumer and producer-durables manufacturing.

REGIONAL TRADE MULTIPLIERS

An indication of the impact of changes in regional trade patterns of the structure and growth of a region can be seen in the size and change of the regional trade multipliers over the two decades. These multipliers are estimated in the same way as metropolitan trade multipliers (See Chapter 4); however, they can be viewed as indexes rather than as actual values.

	1940	1960
New England	6.1	8.0
Middle Atlantic	11.1	12.5
Great Lakes	10.0	9.3
Plains	4.5	6.1
Southeast	3.6	6.3
Southwest	4.3	6.6
Mountain	4.5	5.7
West Coast	6.5	9.1
Pacific	2.6	2.8

As for metropolitan areas, the more developed and the more self-sufficient the economy, the greater the trade multiplier. Hence, we find that the regional impact of changes in trade varies, from 12.5 times in the Middle Atlantic to 2.8 in the Pacific and 5.7 in the Mountain region.

The trade multiplier increases as the region develops and its economy becomes more diversified. In the developing Southeast, the regional trade multiplier doubled over the two decades. In the developed Middle Atlantic region, the multiplier increased, but slightly. The regional trade multiplier increased in all regions except the Great Lakes, a region highly specialized in exporting manufacturing. This suggests that regions, like metropolitan areas, are developing most rapidly in their local sectors and are becoming increasingly self-sufficient.

SUMMARY

In this chapter, regional trade patterns were analyzed in three stages. First, metropolitan trade was divided into its interregional and intraregional components. In most (23 of 30), interregional trade was found to be the more significant portion, and in no industry was it less than 40 percent of metropolitan trade. However, the significance of this finding is limited by the more important earlier finding that trade is a small and declining fraction of total employment (and requirements) in many industries.

Second, the interregional component of metropolitan trade was analyzed to determine if exports were dispersed over several regions or concentrated in a few. Highlights of the industrial analysis of the origins of interregional trade include the following: Over 80 percent of interregional agriculture exports originate in the Southeast or Plains regions; interregional export activity in food and kindred products was concentrated in the Plains; exports of textiles shifted from the New England to the Southeast, which accounted for 86 percent of interregional trade in that industry in 1960; the Great Lakes region dominated interregional trade in motor vehicles, electrical machinery, and miscellaneous manufacturing.

Third, the intraregional component of trade was divided between intercity and city-hinterland forms of trade. Trade between cities was found to dominate the intraregional component in most industries. Typical configurations of the three dimensions of regional trade were illustrated by (1) the lumber and wood products industry, in which exports originate in hinterlands and are found in almost all regions; (2) motor vehicle manufacture, in which exports are concentrated in the metropolitan area of one region; and (3) FIRE, in which exports originate in metropolitan areas of almost all regions and are traded primarily with regional hinterlands and interregional exports are limited to two regions. An examination of changes in regional trade multipliers supported the conclusion that regions, like metropolitan areas, are becoming more self-sufficient.

CHAPTER

7

SPATIAL DYNAMICS
OF EMPLOYMENT
EXPANSION

The changing trade patterns examined in the previous chapter have important implications for the spatial ordering of economic activity. In this chapter those changes in employment, which represent a geographic shift of export activity, are isolated and examined to determine the direction of the shift in each industry.

GEOGRAPHICAL SHIFT OF EXPORT ACTIVITY

In a large, complex economy comprised of 368 essentially separate metropolitan economies and their hinterlands, the measures of trade activity used thus far do not reveal the full extent to which structural changes in trade occur. As was noted in the job-increase-job-decrease analysis, it sometimes happens that production is relocated. Such movement shows up as a job decline in one area and a job increase in another. In examining this phenomenon we will use the term *geographic shift*, defined as job increases in an industry that are offset by declines in the same industry but in other metropolitan places.

Geographical shift of metropolitan exports need not represent an actual shift of production facilities; it may result simply from the diversion of production from export to local markets in some places and, in others, the expansion of production for exports. It may take many forms: from one region to another, from large to small metropolises or from small to large, or from one type of place to another.

An example using data from one industry may help clarify the concept of geographical shift. Increases and decreases in population, requirements, and trade in the motor vehicle industry, 1950-60, for the 368 metropolitan places, are summarized below:

	Increases	Decreases	Geographical Shift	Net Change
Production	104,100	129,300	104,100	-25,200
Requirements	49,200	26,700	26,700	22,500
Exports	74,000	107,300	74,000	-33,300
Imports	48,000	35,500	33,500	12,500

The net decline in metropolitan production of motor vehicles, equivalent to 25,200 jobs, conceals production increases in some places, amounting to 104,100 jobs, as well as about four-fifths of the decreases. Similarly, a net increase in metropolitan imports, equivalent to 12,500 jobs, conceals more than two-thirds (35,500 jobs) of the 48,000 increases in 171 places. Finally, export increases in 39 places, representing 74,000 jobs, were more than offset by declines in other places, amounting to 107,300 jobs—a shift not registered in the net decline of 33,300 jobs.

Geographical shift in the motor vehicle industry is clearly discernible from the data; 73 percent of the job decreases in export activity were offset by job increases in other places. These increases represent roughly 14 percent of the total metropolitan employment in motor vehicles in 1960.

The figures from the motor vehicle industry illustrate two types of geographic shift. First there was a geographic shift in production, which amounted to 104,000 jobs. Second, there was a geographic shift in export activity, which amounted to 74,000 jobs. Geographic shift in production has been anlyzed in an earlier study.[1] The present study is confined to an analysis of the shift in export activity.

Table 7.1 provides data on the actual metropolitan employment in export activity and the percent of that export employment that shifted for each decade. This latter figure, the share of export activity at the start of a decade that had been shifted by the end of it, is referred to as geographic shift of export activity (GSEA).

GSEA among the 30 industries ranged from 40.7 to 0.7 percent during the 1950s. GSEA tended to be relatively more important in locally oriented industries. However, export activity in these industries generally accounts for only a small share of employment, so the high GSEA may be misleading.

The importance of GSEA increased considerably in certain industries—in motor vehicles, from 2,845 jobs (0.7 percent) in the 1940s to 73,901 jobs (13.6 percent) in the 1950s; in electrical and other machinery, from 8,815 to 94,634 jobs (from 2.0 to 12.3 percent); and in medical, educational, and other professional services, from 10,271 to 61,200 (from 5.7 to 17.1 percent). GSEA declined in trucking and warehousing, chemicals and allied products, other transportation equipment, and apparel manufacturing.

THE DIRECTIONS OF GEOGRAPHIC SHIFT

GSEA provides a measure of over-all shift in export activity, but it tells very little about the direction of the shifts. It is important to determine the

79

TABLE 7.1

Geographic Shift of Export Activity

Industry	Metropolitan Exports 1940	GSEA 1940-50 (percent)	Metropolitan Exports 1950	GSEA 1950-60 (percent)
Primary				
Agriculture	318,368	12.5	263,936	10.8
Forestry, fisheries	16,423	12.6	21,121	13.1
Mining	220,755	12.3	205,047	10.9
Construction	140,871	14.7	271,598	25.9
Manufacturing				
Food, kindred products	200,064	8.0	252,589	14.2
Textile mills	485,219	5.6	500,719	2.7
Apparel manufacturing	325,872	7.0	415,691	7.4
Lumber manufacturing	112,659	12.1	128,496	11.3
Printing, publishing	140,061	2.2	190,766	7.8
Chemicals, allied	134,398	12.7	192,507	8.3
Electrical, other machinery	432,915	2.0	769,633	12.3
Motor vehicles, equipment	387,975	0.7	545,003	13.6
Other transportation equipment	156,453	22.3	242,011	16.0
Other miscellaneous manufacturing	1,034,234	3.9	1,243,397	8.3
Utilities	54,814	40.9	51,530	34.8
Mainly Business Services				
Railroad, railway express	207,642	53	264,011	2.1
Trucking, warehousing	30,394	21.8	55,245	9.9
Other transportation	154,643	6.6	218,760	10.6
Communications	59,226	7.1	96,446	17.1
Wholesale	186,511	7.3	312,683	14.3
FIRE	334,286	1.5	403,217	6.3
Business, repair services	56,127	10.9	78,734	16.6
Mainly Consumer Services				
Food, dairy stores	69,442	25.4	60,991	19.9
Eating, drinking places	112,105	16.8	130,309	9.0
Other retail	210,466	9.5	294,606	17.1
Hotel, other personal services	183,183	15.1	181,517	20.3
Entertainment, recreation	68,495	12.0	71,848	12.0
Medical, other professions	181,598	5.7	358,186	17.1
Government				
Public administration	213,355	11.3	464,106	9.2
Armed forces	188,729	10.9	580,463	12.2
Total	6,417,283	7.8	8,865,166	11.5

Source: Based on trade estimates made by using the value added approach described in the text. See Table 3.2.

extent of shift in export activity between metropolitan and non-metropolitan areas, between cities of different sizes, between regions of the nation, and between cities (or between cities and hinterlands) within the same region.

Shift from Metropolitan to Non-metropolitan Areas

Shift from metropolitan to non-metropolitan areas can be detected in the form of decreases in exports from metropolitan areas to hinterlands, which are offset by declining imports and/or emergence of exports in the same industry in non-metropolitan areas.

Metropolitan exports to non-metropolitan areas declined in 16 of the 20 categories in which metropolitan areas had been net exporters at the beginning of the 1950s. In seven of these declining categories, export activity shifted to non-metropolitan areas to such an extent that they became net exporters. The shift is quite striking, involving approximately 711,000 jobs, of which about half represent import replacement. The industrial distribution of jobs shifting from metropolitan to rural areas, along with the industry's VAPE index (VAPE as a percent of national average), is presented below:

New Non-metropolitan Exporters	Number of Jobs Shifted	VAPE Index
Food and kindred products	87,000	107
Apparel	146,000	63
Utilities and sanitary services	33,000	226
Educational, medical, and other professional services	93,000	80
Eating and drinking places	70,000	71
Other retailing	221,000	71
Hotels and other personal services	61,000	55
Total	711,000	81

VAPE in these seven categories averaged 19 percent below the national figure in 1960. Only the relatively few gains in utilities are significantly above average. In contrast, VAPE in the four industries in which net metropolitan exports expanded by 142,000 jobs—printing and publishing, other transportation equipment, FIRE, and business and repair services—averaged 18 percent above the national average. It appears, then, that as jobs in low-VAPE export activity shift toward non-metropolitan areas, exports in high-VAPE industries expand within metropolitan areas.

Shifts Between Size-of-Place Categories

Shift of trade activity between metropolitan areas of different sizes can be detected in decreases in export activity in an industry in places within one size

81

group, which are offset by increases in export activity in places within another size group. However, shifts between metropolitan areas within the same size categories will not be revealed with the available data. Data relating to changes in export activity by the three (large, medium, small) groups of cities are presented in Table 7.2 for the period 1950-60.

The shifts in export activity among different-sized metropolitan areas, combined with the positive correlation between size of place, VAPE, and the size of the trade multiplier (see Chapter 4), suggest that metropolitan areas grow by diversifying their export sectors through the addition of new functions that are "passed down" from larger places. These functions generally represent an improvement in VAPE for the new exporter but are drawn from the lower end of the range of VAPE in the (larger) cities from which they have shifted. This appears to be the case in the transfer of apparel from larger cities to non-metropolitan areas and in the shift of some service activity from medium to smaller areas. The net result of these shifts is a gain in average VAPE for both areas, but the relative positions of the areas remain the same. However, while VAPE in non-metropolitan areas remains lowest, the gap between rural and metropolitan areas is narrowing as indicated in declining ETOT for all metropolitan areas, and the gap between ETOT for different size of place categories is also narrowing (See Chapter 5).

Shifts Between Regions

Shift of export activity between regions can be detected by increased exports in one industry in a region offset by declines in the same industry in another region. An industrial breakdown of changes in regional exports is presented for 1950-60 in Table 7.3. These data refer to changes in interregional trade and do not include intraregional shifts. (In interpreting Table 7.3, one should keep in mind that interregional trade is only a fraction of total metropolitan trade and that the significance of interregional trade is declining.)

The major shifts in interregional exports appear toward the Southeast. The region gained export employment in apparel manufacture, offsetting declines in the Middle Atlantic region. It gained also in textiles, offsetting declines in New England. Other shifts that are observable in Table 7.3 are gains in mining exports in two western regions offset by declines in the Southeast, and a shift in the other miscellaneous manufacturing category from the Northeast regions to the Great Lakes.

Intraregional Shifts

Intraregional shifts of export activity are more important than inter-regional shifts. These shifts can be detected as increases within an industry in one portion of the region (either a metropolitan or the non-metropolitan area), offset by declines in another (either another metropolis or the non-metropolitan

TABLE 7.2

Measures of Metropolitan Shift of Exports, 1950-60
(employment, thousands)

Industry	Code	Large	Medium	Small
Primary				
Agriculture	1			
Forestry and fisheries	2			−30
Mining	3			8
Construction	4		−4	8
Manufacturing				
Food, kindred products	5		−42	5
Textile mills	6		−12	20
Apparel	7	−84		
Lumber	8			−3
Printing, publishing	9	8	2	
Chemical	10	−8	−3	2
Electrical, other machinery	11	95	−108	1
Motor vehicle equipment	12	−65	7	
Other transportation equipment	13	−8	64	
Other miscellaneous manufacturing	14	−85	−54	−7
Utilities	19	−1	−7	2
Mainly Business Services				
Railroad, railway express	15		−29	−19
Trucking, warehousing	16		8	4
Other transportation	17	1	−12	
Communications	18	−12	6	
Wholesale	20	−19	10	
FIRE	24		28	
Business, repair	27	101		
Mainly Consumer Services				
Food, dairy product stores	21			−2
Eating, drinking places	22	−17	−8	
Other retail	23		−64	12
Hotel, other personal services	25	−3	−22	10
Entertainment, recreation	28	1		
Medical, education	29			37
Government				
Administration	30	−41	−9	
Armed forces	31		−15	94

Source: Based on trade estimates made by using the value added approach described in the text. See Table 3.2.

TABLE 7.3

Changes in Interregional Export Trade, 1950-60
(employment equivalents, thousands)

Industry	New England	Middle Atlantic	Great Lakes
Primary			
Agriculture			
Forestry and fisheries	−3.4		
Mining			
Construction			
Manufacturing			
Food, kindred products			−20.1
Textile mills	−113.6		
Apparel	3.5	−59.4	
Lumber			
Printing, publishing	3.3	17.7	13.2
Chemical		11.1	0.4
Electrical, other machinery	32.8	23.3	51.7
Motor vehicle equipment			−32.3
Other transportation equipment	35.1		−17.7
Other miscellaneous manufacturing	−8.0	−54.2	15.0
Utilities		−1.4	
Mainly Business Services			
Railroad, railway express			15.8
trucking, warehousing			8.1
Other transportation		5.1	
Communications		−2.5	
Wholesale		−5.3	
FIRE	−2.1	−9.0	
Business repair		31.7	
Mainly Consumer Services			
Food, dairy product stores		−18.1	
Eating, drinking places			
Other retail			
Hotel, other personal services			
Entertainment, recreation		1.7	
Medical, education	2.4	−9.0	
Government			
Administration		5.2	
Armed forces			

Plains	Southeast	Southwest	Rocky Mountains	Far West	Pacific
−179.7	−791.3	−109.5	−21.4		−6.0
	−8.8		2.0	−2.6	−2.3
	−72.7	35.5	6.5		
−8.3	95.2	−8.6	−2.4	−54.4	3.6
10.4			0.6	−14.7	3.0
	43.0				
	59.4				
	−54.1			−11.8	
3.5					
	18.5				
				103.1	−2.4
3.8	10.7	9.2	0.8	−11.7	−0.3
−9.8	−4.0		−8.4		
−1.7		2.4	1.7		
	17.5	−0.4		−0.7	1.9
1.2		−4.6	0.3	−0.7	
−8.6		16.9	2.0	−18.2	
		3.1		1.1	
−21.1		7.5	−6.7	23.3	
	22.5	4.9			
4.4		−7.4	3.1	−19.4	0.4
13.2	129.5	15.1	3.8	−63.7	
	39.0	5.1	2.2	−13.0	1.3
		−1.5	−0.5	5.9	
39.8		0.7	11.7	−16.4	−1.8
	28.9	17.9	10.0	−9.5	2.0
	93.1	42.8		27.6	34.2

Source: Based on trade estimates made by using the value added approach described in the text. See Table 3.2.

TABLE 7.4

Intraregional Shift in Metropolitan Trade, 1950-60

Industry	Intraregional Shift Total	Percent GSEA
Primary		
Agriculture	19,544	68.6
Forestry and fisheries	1,999	72.4
Mining	11,235	32.5
Construction	48,871	69.4
Manufacturing		
Food, kindred products	21,217	59.0
Textile mills	13,690	99.7
Apparel	13,356	43.3
Lumber	14,119	97.4
Printing, publishing	8,913	60.0
Chemical	15,641	98.4
Electrical, other machinery	90,775	95.9
Motor vehicle equipment	55,772	75.5
Other transportation equipment	24,715	63.9
Other miscellaneous manufacturing	91,334	88.1
Utilities	8,222	45.8
Mainly Business Services		
Railroad, railway express	5,592	100.0
Trucking, warehousing	5,445	100.0
Other transportation	17,542	75.7
Communications	11,221	68.1
Wholesale	26,360	58.8
FIRE	22,471	88.9
Business, repair	9,326	71.4
Mainly Consumer Services		
Food, dairy product stores	8,052	66.4
Eating, drinking places	11,404	97.2
Other retail	30,404	60.2
Hotel, other personal services	29,470	80.0
Entertainment, recreation	6,997	81.3
Medical, education	55,049	90.0
Government		
Administration	35,818	84.1
Armed forces	68,281	96.2

Percent Distribution of Intraregional Shift							
New England	Middle Atlantic	Great Lakes	Plains	Southeast	Southwest	Rocky Mountains	Far West
	0.1	12.7	14.8	10.6	26.6		35.0
7.8		2.1	0.9	30.5	14.1		44.8
	1.3	3.4	1.6	60.6	10.7	22.3	
0.9	1.4	0.1	6.1	37.9	17.9	6.3	27.3
	16.5	28.9	12.8	9.5	9.4	3.0	15.0
1.9	4.4	1.3		92.4			
21.1	72.3		1.5	3.4	1.7		
1.8	1.5	14.5	0.3	29.6	4.1		48.3
0.5	31.8	36.7	15.9	3.3	2.1	1.2	8.4
11.4	28.6	7.7	4.1	43.5	4.6		
9.6	33.6	47.5	9.3				
	3.0	95.5	1.5				
16.5	33.7	29.9		7.3	3.5		9.0
20.2	25.1		3.0	15.2	2.2	0.5	
0.2	20.4	13.7	7.7	28.4	15.4	7.0	7.1
0.8	40.3	43.6	1.1	2.7	1.2	1.1	9.2
2.5	5.0	17.8	24.7	1.9	19.2	3.4	25.6
	54.7	0.4	4.7	25.6	9.8		4.8
0.4	10.1	9.9	13.2	18.2	20.5	5.8	21.9
0.9	9.0	8.0	10.3	32.2	15.5	1.7	22.4
7.1	60.1	11.3	6.2	0.9	4.3		10.1
7.2	9.9	9.3	4.1	12.3	13.8	13.6	29.9
3.2	19.1	9.1	5.7	41.6	12.8	0.9	7.6
	3.9	23.6	10.3	37.2	5.1	5.3	14.5
0.6	6.9	13.8	8.7	36.8	18.1	2.9	12.3
0.7	1.1	2.0	3.1	40.9	11.4	2.2	38.7
	1.4	1.3	8.1	43.1	8.0	1.5	36.5
3.0	38.0	2.4	3.0	9.2	2.8	2.1	39.5
4.7	2.7	4.6	3.2	22.2	18.4	4.8	39.4
1.4	10.3	1.2		4.9	16.4	11.3	54.5

Source: Based on trade estimates made by using the value added approach described in the text. See Table 3.2.

area). A complete analysis of intraregional shift would distinguish between intermetropolitan shifts, suburbanization, and shifts between metropolis and hinterland. Such an analysis was not undertaken here, but Table 7.4 does present data on intraregional shift.

The most important observation for Table 7.4 is that intraregional shifts far outnumber interregional shifts in export activity. Over-all intraregional shifts were 89 percent of all shifts (GSEA). Intraregional shifts were dominant in every industry but three—mining, apparel, and utilities.

The main factors in intraregional redistribution of an industry are, of course, the extent to which its export activity is regionally concentrated and the extent to which it is shifting to non-metropolitan areas. In medical, education, and other professional services, which are regionally dispersed, intraregional shift was significant in all regions in the U.S. and accounted for 90 percent of geographic shift in the industry. In motor vehicles, however, where trade activity is concentrated in the Great Lakes, 95 percent in intraregional shift was in that region.

Intraregional shift, which accounts for so much of all geographic shift, certainly requires further analysis in future studies. The changing spatial configuration of export activity (and, in fact, all employment activity) within a region is an important aspect of urban economics that remains largely unexplored.[2]

GEOGRAPHIC CONCENTRATION OF TRADE

Another way to view shifts in trade activity is to ask whether they contribute to concentration or dispersion of trade activity. We have already noted in Chapter 5 that in most industries production is becoming more dispersed and that trade accounts for a decreasing proportion of total employment. Nonetheless, the absolute level of employment in trade activity is increasing, and it is important to determine if this employment is becoming more or less concentrated.

Since no single measure of concentration is adequate, two analyses will be utilized: the percentage of places exporting related to the precentage of total employment engaged in export activity in each industry; and the percentage of trade activity accounted for by the three largest exporters in each industry.

In general, it is expected that there is an inverse relationship between the percentage of places exporting and the percentage of employment in export ac-tivity. When an industry is established, production is concentrated in a few places and exports are a large part of total production. As time passes, exports usually account for a smaller share of output, as production is dispersed and there is an increase in the number of exporting places. The relationship, when plotted for a given year, should resemble a rectangular hyperbola: Increases in the percentage of places exporting (moving from left to right along the curve) tend to become larger with each decline in the relative importance of export activity.

The actual relationship is plotted in Chart 7.1 for 1940 and 1960 for each industrial category. In both years the hypothesized over-all pattern of

88

CHART 7.1

Geographic Concentration of Metropolitan Exports

1940 (+) and 1960 (•)

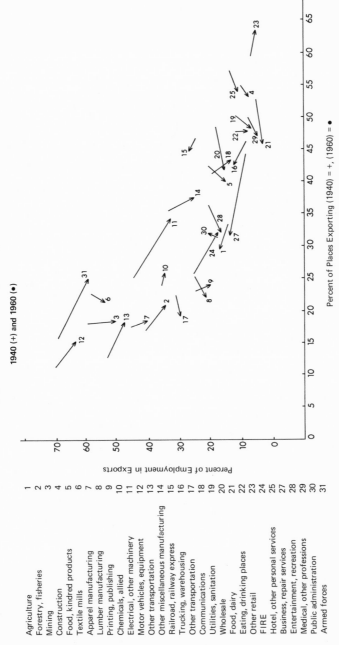

Percent of Employment in Exports

Percent of Places Exporting (1940) = +, (1960) = •

Source: Based on trade estimates made by using the value added approach described in the text. See Table 3.2.

1	Agriculture
2	Forestry, fisheries
3	Mining
4	Construction
5	Food, kindred products
6	Textile mills
7	Apparel manufacturing
8	Lumber manufacturing
9	Printing, publishing
10	Chemicals, allied
11	Electrical, other machinery
12	Motor vehicles, equipment
13	Other transportation
14	Other miscellaneous manufacturing
15	Railroad, railway express
16	Trucking, warehousing
17	Other transportation
18	Communications
19	Utilities, sanitation
20	Wholesale
21	Food, dairy
22	Eating, drinking places
23	Other retail
24	FIRE
25	Hotel, other personal services
27	Business, repair services
28	Entertainment, recreation
29	Medical, other professions
30	Public administration
31	Armed forces

89

relationships is observed, but in each industry there is some change in the relationship over the 20-year period. In interpreting the graph we should note the following:

1. A decrease in percent of employment engaged in export activity accompanied by an increase in percentage of places exporting indicates a decline in the concentration of export activity.

2. An increase in percent of employment engaged in export activity accompanied by a decrease in percentage of places exporting indicates an increase in the concentration of economic activity.

3. A decrease in percent of employment engaged in export activity accompanied by a decrease in percentage of places exporting represents an anomalous situation: There is concentration of trade activity, but in relation to a diminished base. Concentration does not necessarily represent increased economic activity.

4. An increase in percent of employment engaged in export accompanied by an increase in percentage of places exporting is an inconclusive finding. One cannot say whether or not there has been a greater concentration in economic activity.

Analysis of Chart 7.1 can be summarized by grouping the types of change.

Decreased concentration:
(Percentage of employment in trade [-], percentage of places exporting [+])

> Primary:
> > Forestry and fisheries
> Manufacturing:
> > Apparel manufacturing
> > Printing and publishing
> > Chemical and allied
> > Electrical and other machinery
> > Motor vehicles and equipment
> > Other transportation equipment
> > Other and miscellaneous
> Mainly business services:
> > Communications
> > FIRE
> Mainly consumer services:
> > Other retail
> Armed forces

Increased concentration:
(Percentage of employment in trade [+], percentage of places exporting [-])

> Agriculture
> Mainly business services:
> > Trucking and warehousing
> > Business and repair services
> > Railroad and railway express

Decreased number of places exporting but smaller percentage employment in trade:

> Contract construction
> Manufacturing:
>> Food and kindred
>> Textile mill products
>> Lumber manufacturing
> Utilities
> Mainly business services:
>> Other transportation
>> Communications
>> Wholesale
> Mainly consumer services:
>> Food and dairy stores
>> Eating and drinking places
>> Hotels and other personal services
>> Entertainment and recreation
>> Med., education

Evidence inconclusive:

> Mining
> Public administration

From this summary we observe a decrease in concentration in most of the manufacturing classifications and in armed services, where traditionally there has been a relatively high percentage of employment engaged in export production, as well as in two service classifications, FIRE and other retail. The latter represent financial services and specialty retailing, which have traditionally been exported in part from major trading centers and which are being dispersed among metropolitan economies with growth and rising income levels (that is, passed down the hierarchy of places).

Clearly defined concentration trends are noted only in agriculture and in three business services, trucking and warehousing, railroads and railway express, and business-repair services. Here there has, presumably, been some tendency for increased specialization in nodal metropolitan centers.

Finally, there is a large number (13) of classifications where there has been a decline in number of places exporting in the face of a decline in trading activity. It is important to note that trade activity is relatively unimportant in each of these classifications. In none does total export activity represent more than 22 percent of the industry's metropolitan employment in 1960 (See Chart 7.1), so it seems inappropriate to regard these changes as representing significant concentrations of trade. There were three industries, however, where percentage of employment in trade was relatively high and the reduction of number of places exporting may be regarded as an increased concentration of trade activity: textile mills, other transportation (largely airline and water), and lumber products.

91

TABLE 7.5

Concentration Analysis

Industry	Percent of Exports in Three Largest Places		
	1940	1960	Change (+) (−)
Primary			
Agriculture	8.7	18.3*	+
Forestry and fisheries	22.2	17.8	−
Mining	38.5	20.6	−
Construction	20.5	12.7	−
Manufacturing			
Food, kindred products	25.0	17.6	−
Textile mills	11.0	21.8*	+
Apparel	67.8	63.9	−
Lumber	20.1	28.5*	+
Printing, publishing	58.2	53.2	−
Chemical	25.9	23.2	−
Electrical, other machinery	25.4	26.2	+
Motor vehicle equipment	79.2	62.5	−
Other transportation equipment	39.1	45.4	+
Other miscellaneous manufacturing	20.1	21.9	+
Utilities	32.0	13.3	−
Mainly Business Services			
Railroad, railway express	16.3	20.3*	+
Trucking, warehousing	15.1	20.7*	+
Other transportation	51.2	58.6*	+
Communications	38.1	38.5	0
Wholesale	21.0	34.6	+
FIRE	52.0	46.4	+
Business, repair	46.2	55.5*	+
Mainly Consumer Services			
Food, dairy product stores	48.0	13.0	−
Eating/drinking places	42.0	28.4	−
Other retail	16.7	11.3	−
Hotel, other personal services	27.5	25.7	−
Entertainment, recreation	75.7	62.6	−
Medical, education	27.4	18.2	−
Government			
Administration	52.7	42.3	−
Armed forces	33.2	23.9	−

*Evidence of increased concentration.

92

Change (+) (−) Percent of Places Exporting, 1940-60	The Three Metropolitan Areas with Largest Share of Total Metropolitan Trade, 1960
−	Fresno (7.2), Hidalgo, Tex. (6.5), Yakima, Wash. (4.6)
+	Fall River (6.3), Missoula, Mont. (6.1), Seattle (5.5)
N.C.	Houston (7.6), Duluth (7.5), Tulsa (5.5)
−	Tampa-St. Pete (5.0), Ft. Laud. (3.9), Houston (3.8)
−	Chicago (8.7), Omaha (4.7), Minn.-St. Paul (4.2)
−	Prov. (7.8), Greenville (7.2), Gastonia (6.8)
+	N.Y. (52.2), Phila. (7.0), Fall River, Mass. (4.7)
−	Eugene, Ore. (11.8), Eureka, Cal. (10.2), Grand Rpds. (6.5)
+	N.Y. (28.5), Chicago (18.5), Phila. (6.2)
+	Wilmington, Del. (9.0), Newark (7.4), Phila. (6.8)
+	Chicago (14.5), Milwaukee (6.0), Boston (5.7)
+	Detroit (45.9), Flint, Mich. (11.1), Cleveland (5.5)
+	L.A. (28.0), Seattle (11.4), Wichita (6.0)
+	Pittsburgh (10.4), Chicago (6.2), Gary (5.3)
−	Houston (5.8), Shreveport (4.4), Memphis/Phoenix (3.1)
−	Chicago (11.9), Pittsburgh (4.3), Altoona, Pa. (4.1)
−	Chicago (10.2), Jersey City (5.4), St. Louis (5.1)
−	N.Y. (41.5), San Francisco (8.9), Miami (8.2)
+	N.Y. (23.6), L.A. (9.7), San Francisco (5.2)
−	N.Y. (26.2), Minn.-St. Paul (4.3), L.A. (4.1)
+	N.Y. (35.0), San Francisco (5.7), L.A. (5.7)
−	N.Y. (31.0), L.A. (18.7), San Francisco (5.8)
−	Boston (4.6), Houston (4.6), Miami (3.8)
+	N.Y. (17.9), Miami (6.7), Ft. Lauderdale (3.8)
+	Tampa-St. Pete (4.4), Miami (4.2), Atlanta (2.7)
−	Miami (10.9), N.Y. (8.6), Las Vegas (6.2)
−	L.A. (38.1), N.Y. (19.7), Las Vegas (4.8)
−	D.C. (7.5), Boston (6.6), N.Y. (4.1)
+	D.C. (33.2), Sacramento (5.1), San Antonio (4.0)
+	San Diego (11.6), Norfolk, Va. (7.3), Honolulu (5.0)

Source: Based on trade estimates made by using the value added approach described in the text. See Table 3.2.

The three largest exporters in each industry. The other measure of concentration is similar to the one often used by economists to study the degree of industrial concentration among firms, the percentage of activity accounted for by the three largest producers. The shares of trade in the three places that accounted for the largest share of exports for the census years 1940 and 1960 are presented in Table 7.5. The table also indicates for each industry whether the percentage of all metropolitan places exporting increased or decreased from 1940 to 1960 (based on Chart 7.1).

The results are similar to those of the previous analysis. In those seven classifications for which evidence of increased export concentration was found (agriculture, textile mills, lumber, railroad/railway express, trucking/ware-housing, other transportation, business-repair services), the percentage of exports in the three largest places increased. In all other industrial classifications except four, the percentage of exports in the three largest places declined or stayed the same. The four industries not classified previously as increasing in export concentration were electrical-other machinery, other transportation equipment, and other-miscellaneous manufactures, where the number of places exporting increased, even though concentration occurred among the top-ranked three places, and wholesaling, where there appears to have been a very considerable concentration among the three leading exporters (from 21 to 35 percent), accompanied by a decline of percentage of places exporting from 48 to 42.

The three places with the largest share of export activity are also listed in Table 7.5. Conventional associations of industries with places are generally confirmed. New York is the leading exporter in apparel, air transportation, business and repair services, printing and publishing, FIRE, communications, and wholesaling. Los Angeles leads in entertainment and recreation, and other transportation (including aircraft and shipping) manufacturing. Chicago leads in electrical and other machinery, trucking and warehousing, railroads and railway express services, and food and kindred products. Detroit leads in motor vehicle manufacturing; Washington, D.C., in public administration; Eugene, Oregon, in lumber and wood products; Miami in hotels (it is second in eating and drinking places and third in transportation services—primarily airlines). San Diego leads in armed forces; Wilmington, Delaware, in chemicals; Providence, Rhode Island, in textiles; and Houston in mining (petroleum).

The extent to which export activity is concentrated in the three places with largest shares is influenced primarily by the share accounted for by the first largest exporter. For example, among the 10 industries with largest shares of exports accounted for by the top three places in 1960, the share of total metropolitan exports in the largest exporting place ranges from 52 to 24 percent; the share in the third largest, from 8 to 4 percent. Thus, the share of exports in the second and third largest exporting places dropped off rapidly in the most concentrated industries.

Although the export sector of metropolitan economies is generally diversified, in roughly one-third of all metropolitan places (145), a single industry category accounted for over half of the place's export activity. The dominance of one exporting industry makes these areas extremely vulnerable to cyclical, seasonal, or policy changes (private or public) that affect production in the industries in which they specialize. Indeed, the economic health and growth of the entire metropolis rests primarily on events in one industry or decisions made in one corporate headquarters office or government agency. Moreover, such a place may well have difficulty in attracting new industries. The labor force is probably highly specialized and the interests of the dominant industry may supersede all other community interests. Locational barriers to entry may also involve poor or imperfect information concerning local labor markets, unavailability of producer services, including poor prospects of local financing, and inadequate social infrastructure—schools, hospitals, roads, fire and police protection.

Three industrial classifications stand out as tending to dominate export sectors in metropolitan areas: other miscellaneous manufacturing, dominant in 29 places; armed forces, in 24; and electrical and other machinery, in 19. Miscellaneous manufacturing includes a broad group of industries not specifically defined, but many of the places in which this category is dominant specialize in a single subindustry category. Together these three categories account for 72 of the 145 places whose export sectors are dominated by one industry.

NEW YORK—CAPITAL OF THE NATION'S BUSINESS

At the apex of the national urban system's hierarchy of cities and a leader in international trade and finance, New York is a metropolis that requires special attention.[3] New York accounts for the largest share of metropolitan export activity in 8 of the 13 most geographically concentrated industries. In 1960, it supplied over half of all metropolitan exports in apparel and the largest share of trade in all five business service categories: 42 percent of other transportation, 35 percent of FIRE, 31 percent of business and repair services, 26 percent of wholesaling, and 24 percent of communications. New York also accounts for the largest share of export employment in printing and publishing (29 percent) and eating and drinking places (18 percent) and is second only to Los Angeles in recreation and entertainment and to Miami in hotels and personal services.

It is this intense concentration of metropolitan trade activity in the New York metropolitan region that constitutes its main locational advantage. It is the major transportation and communications center in the nation, as well as the site of the major money markets and headquarters of many of the nation's largest corporations, trade associations, and foundations. Related activities such as advertising, engineering, consulting, and educational, legal, and accounting services also agglomerate within the city.

Further study would probably show that a large share of New York's employment in mining, apparel, printing and publishing, and other manufacturing and service categories represents regional or national offices of major corporations. Indeed, one can hardly analyze the New York economy without considering corporate headquarters activity as a separate industry category. The locational attractions of New York, including the sophisticated infrastructure of business and consumer services and amenities, apply to all corporate headquarters activities, regardless of industry. Space and manpower requirements are also similar in this activity regardless of industry; office space is typically found in high-rise buildings, and the work force is comprised primarily of white-collar and professional workers. Indeed, New York's future growth will depend primarily on its ability to maintain the locational advantages it can offer these headquarters activities.

The economy is exceptionally dynamic. Of the many businesses "incubated" there, a number in time outgrew the city. Many older industries have left New York; in fact, the United Nations now stands on a site previously occupied by earlier "nuisance industries." The fashion industry, however, which predates most other activities in New York, remains.

TABLE 7.6

New York City's Share of Total Metropolitan Trade in Selected Industries

Industry	1940	1960
Apparel	56.3	52.2
Airlines and other transportation	36.6	41.5
FIRE	40.6	35.0
Business and repair services	24.8	31.0
Printing and publishing	28.6	28.5
Wholesaling	6.8	26.2
Communications	19.7	23.6
Entertainment and recreation	23.7	19.7
Eating and drinking places	17.9	17.9
Hotels and other personal services	17.5	8.6
Medical and other professional services	13.3	4.1

Source: Based on trade estimates made by using the value added approach described in the test. See Table 3.2.

As Table 7.6 shows, the advantages resulting from the concentration of such a wide range of specialized activities and a large and diversified labor force do not seem to have eroded over the period examined. New York's share of metropolitan trade activity actually increased in four of the above industry categories. Increased dominance of exports in business and repair services and other transportation services is particularly significant since total metropolitan export activity expanded rapidly in these industries, 142 and 10 percent, respectively.

SUMMARY

Analysis of the job increases and decreases (summarized in chapter 5) indicated that in each industry some portion of the changes represented a shift of export activity from one place to another. Over-all, geographic shift of export activity (GSEA) represented 8 percent of all metropolitan export employment in the first decade and 12 percent in the second. In almost all industries, most of the shift was within regions, but there was significant interregional shift in mining, apparel, and utilities. Shift of export activity between metropolitan areas of different sizes and between metropolitan and non-metropolitan areas pointed to a "passing down" of functions from larger areas to smaller areas, with most of the shifts yielding a relative rise in average productivity for the new exporting place.

Additional analysis of shifts in export activity provided evidence of increased geographic concentration of export activity in seven industries—agriculture, trucking and warehousing, business and repair services, other transportation, textiles, electrical machinery, and lumber manufacturing. In the remaining manufacturing classifications, there was either evidence of decreased concentration of export activity or no conclusive evidence of a trend in either direction.

NOTES

1. See Thomas M. Stanback and Richard V. Knight, *The Metropolitan Economy: The Process of Employment Expansion* (New York: Columbia University Press, 1970), chapter 9.

2. The Conservation of Human Resources Project is presently engaged in a study of suburbanization and employment activity, one important aspect of intraregional shifts.

3. The Conservation of Human Resources staff has explored many aspects of the New York labor market in their *New York Is Very Much Alive: A Manpower View* (New York: McGraw-Hill, 1973).

CHAPTER

8

KEY FINDINGS
AND IMPLICATIONS

The value added approach was developed in order to measure trade and to determine the employment-related consequences of changes in trade activity. This final chapter is an effort to synthesize the findings of each previous chapter and highlight the trends that emerge from the analyses.

KEY FINDINGS

One major trend that characterizes the period 1940-60, especially during the second decade, is the increasing self-sufficiency of metropolitan economies. Metropolitan areas produce more of their own requirements and depend less on trade to meet their needs. The increase is apparent in a variety of ways. Metropolitan trade multipliers increased substantially over each decade, indicating an expanded local sector. Employment in export activity declined as a percentage of total metropolitan employment; metropolitan areas imported a decreasing percentage of their requirements. Yet another way in which self-sufficiency became apparent is that growth in production for local demand was much more important than expanded export activity in over-all employment increases; this was particularly true in the 1950s. In general, the increased demand brought about by rising per capita income was concentrated in activities that metropolitan areas were best suited to produce locally. Hence, growth was concentrated in the local sector, and a smaller percentage of total requirements had to be imported.

Increased self-sufficiency characterized virtually every type of area, though the trend was more pronounced in some than in others. Self-sufficiency increased in all size categories but most in the places already most self-sufficient. The share of employment in the local sector increased 3.3

98

percentage points in the large category, 2.3 points in the medium-sized category, and only 1.3 points in the small class. Similarly, the percent of community requirements that were imported declined 9.8, 5.8, and 2.1 percentage points in the large, medium, and small categories, respectively. Increased self-sufficiency was also apparent on a regional level. In every region except one, regional trade multipliers became larger over the period reviewed.

A second major finding is that although self-sufficiency is on the rise, trade remains a significant phenomenon. The equivalent of over 11.1 million workers were engaged in producing goods that were imported by metropolitan areas in 1960. Application of the value added approach revealed the significant characteristics of trade activity. Trade is primarily between metropolitan areas; of the more than 11 million jobs in the production of goods or services imported by cities, over 7 million are in one metropolitan area that supplies goods or services to another. Trade between metropolitan and non-metropolitan areas has declined significantly; while in 1940 metropolitan imports from non-metropolitan areas required over 5 million workers, by 1960 the figure had dropped to 3.65 million. In most industry categories trade was found to be predominantly interregional in nature, with relatively little trade between areas in a region. Of the trade that was intraregional, the greatest portion was between cities in the same region.

Trade in services is almost as important as trade in goods. Services, increasing between 1940 and 1960 from 36 to 44 percent of total metropolitan employment in export activity, can no longer be viewed as a localized activity. Nor can trade in services be considered simply as exports from metropolis to surrounding non-metropolitan areas. In 1960, about one-third of all metropolitan service requirements were imported, primarily from other cities.

The analyses of changing trade patterns provided an insight into how the process of growth and increased self-sufficiency operates. It was found that diversification and upgrading (that is, higher VAPE) of the export sector were important sources of growth, and employment expansion does not occur only as a result of expanding traditional export activities. The upgrading of export activity brings greater income into a community and stimulates demand for local services; this in turn generates growth in the local sector, increases the multiplier, and produces greater self-sufficiency.

The increasing significance of changes in trade multipliers was evident in a regression analysis based on the assumption of static multiplier relationships. The regression explained only 68 percent of the variation in growth rates for the 1950s compared to 84 percent in the 1940s. The importance of diversity and upgrading in expanding the trade multiplier was evident in another regression analysis, in which productivity of the export sector and diversity of the export sector, along with size of place, were able to explain three-quarters of the variation in the multiplier statistic. The case study of Huntsville, Alabama, also illustrated the significance of upgrading in the export sector; between 1950 and 1960 total employment in Huntsville grew by over 20,000, but export employment had a net growth of only 600. An expanded local sector was made possible by the transition from primary sector exports to higher productivity NASA-related activity.

Finally, the analysis of shifts in trade activity provides evidence that upgrading of export activity results in part from a "passing down" of functions from larger areas to smaller ones. Low-productivity export industries have relocated from large and medium-sized metropolitan areas to small metropolitan areas and non-metropolitan counties. In the apparel industry, for example, 32 percent of metropolitan exports were for non-metropolitan markets in 1940, but by 1960 metropolitan areas had become net importers, and 12 percent of their imports came from non-metropolitan areas. Similarly, in the textile industry alone 191,000 jobs were shifted from metropolitan to non-metropolitan areas between 1940 and 1960; net imports of textiles increased from 9 to 58 percent of total metropolitan requirements. The shift of exports from metropolitan to non-metropolitan areas is quite striking, involving about a million jobs in 12 industry categories with an average productivity level 29 percent below the national average. This shift offset about one-third of the export jobs in the primary sector in non-metropolitan areas, a sector that had even lower average productivity.

In contrast, productivity in the four industries in which net metropolitan exports expanded by 142,000 jobs—printing and publishing, other transportation equipment, FIRE, and business and repair services—averaged 18 percent above the national average. It appears, then, that as jobs in low-productivity areas are shifted toward non-metropolitan areas, exports in high-productivity industries expand within metropolitan areas. In fact, selective shifts of industries have effected a general increase in productivity in all areas. Thus, average productivity increased in places of all sizes and in non-metropolitan areas, although the relative position of each remained constant with some narrowing of differentials. The employment terms of trade (ETOT) for large areas was greater than all other size categories in both 1940 and 1960, but dropped from 151 to 120 over the period. At the other end of the hierarchy, non-metropolitan areas had the least favorable ETOT throughout the period, but the ratio rose from 35 to 48.

The diversification of the local sector, its increasing self-sufficiency, the changing industrial composition and geographical shift of export activity, and the rise of services—in short, the new metropolism—began to show marked effects on the process of employment expansion during the fifties. Declining export activity accounted for almost half (44 percent) of total job decreases in the 1950s compared to one-fifth (22 percent) during the 1940s. Moreover, the share of job increases attributable to increased export activity fell from 26 to 19 percent, and the share attributable to import substitutions rose from 6 to 9 percent. Job increases related to production for local demand rose from 71 to 76 percent. In short, changes in trade activity accounted for a larger share of job decreases and a smaller share of job increases, and, as a result, the share of metropolitan employment attributable to export activity fell from 20.9 percent in 1940 to 18.5 percent in 1960.

The findings summarized above provide a general outline of changes that occurred in the spatial organization of the U.S. economy over two decades, 1940-60. Inasmuch as they are based on estimates on net trade activity, they are subject to a certain degree of error (described in Chapter 3). The estimates could be improved by increasing the number of industrial classifications and by

100

allowing for local variations in industry productivity, net flow of funds between communities, and international trade. The trends are so clear, however, that improved estimates are not likely to alter the findings significantly.

IMPLICATIONS OF THE STUDY

This study demonstrates the usefulness of analyzing the spatial dynamics of employment growth within the framework of a national system of urban economies linked together through trade. Incorporating the spatial dimension enhances our understanding of economic growth in four ways: First, employment change is seen as far more extensive than traditional aggregate (national and regional) analyses would suggest. Secondly, the local sectors of metropolitan economies are identified as the major source of employment expansion. Thirdly, changing patterns of metropolitan export activity suggest that metropolitan labor markets are continuously being upgraded by taking on new functions and spinning off older ones and, further, that functions are usually passed down the regional hierarchy of labor markets, although in some cases regional shift is involved. Finally, differences in metropolitan growth rates can be explained to a large extent by changes in export activity and their impact on the local sector.

The spatial dimension does count and should be incorporated into economic models and taken into consideration by policy-makers. The national economy does not exist at a point in space, as implied in macroaggregate analyses, but at many interrelated and competing points (urban labor markets) that differ greatly in size, type of exports, and growth rates. Macro-models attempt to explain only net change, which represents just the tip of the iceberg. When the spatial dimension is taken into account, changes that would be netted out in macro-analyses are found to be even more significant than the net change that is examined in macro-analyses. Should policy be based on net changes or gross changes in the economy? Obviously, more attention must be given to the subnational adjustments that are involved in achieving a given change in national aggregates. Similarly, we should take into account the differential impact that changes in national policies have at different points in the national urban system. The impact may differ not only in degree but also in direction, especially as effects are traced out through time and space. In short, too much is expected from national econometric models. To increase our understanding of the economy and hence the effectiveness of policy measures, we will have to specify relationships between and within subnational or metropolitan economies. This study suggests some general guidelines as to how we may best proceed.

A major implication of the study is that we should distinguish between the growth of the local sector of metropolitan economies and changes in its export activity—that is, changes in the structural relationships within the national urban system. The relative importance of the local sector in terms of employment opportunities is increasing over time, and the nature of this

101

change is relatively predictable in terms of (1) the characteristics of the metropolitan area (productivity and diversity of the export sector and size of place), (2) changes in the export base, and (3) changes in the national parameters of industry productivity and demand. While the analyses reported here are of an exploratory nature, they do indicate that the growth process of the local sector would be relatively easy to analyze. Although the local sector accounts for three-quarters of job increases, very little research has been focused on the growth processes involved.

Changes in the pattern of export activity will be more difficult to explain, but some components can be readily analyzed. National trends in export activity can be accounted for (and forecast) in terms of industry demand, productivity, foreign competition, and share of employment in export activity. Changes in the share of employment in export activity in an industry will depend on the trend in geographical dispersion or concentration and on the extent of import substitution in expanding metropolitan and regional markets. The geographical shift of export activity is more difficult to analyze. The first step is accurately to describe changes that have occurred; analyses begun in this study could be continued, using more detailed industry classification. The next step is to identify the nature of the shift: whether it is between labor markets of different sizes or types, within or between regions, and so on. Examining the characteristics of places that are new exporters in an industry, of places where exports are increasing or decreasing, or of those that are no longer exporting would give us considerable information about the nature of geographical shifts.[1]

If we were able to identify the reasons for geographical shift, such as changes in technology, transportation, taxes, wages, markets, and so on, we would be in a better position to anticipate the extent and nature of future shifts. Present practice is to forecast a local industry's growth by projecting the surrounding area's share of national production. This production does not allow for metropolitan trade's changing share of national activity or for geographical shift in export activity. These two trends, even roughly approximated, when applied to national projections of activity in each industry, will indicate the type of basic restructuring that will occur in the national urban system over the coming decades. These rudimentary steps would take us some distance toward understanding the spatial dynamics of economic development. Moreover, once the national urban system is modeled satisfactorily, the model could be used to assess the impact of expected or proposed changes in national parameters or policies.

Specification of changes in national and regional patterns of trade activity would provide metropolitan labor markets with a basis for understanding the changes occurring in their own economies. One reason for emphasizing the metropolitan trade trends and the effect that the growth of a metropolis has on the competitiveness of its export industries is that changes in trade are amplified through the multiplier effect, which varies by place. The number of jobs added (or lost) in the local sector for every 100 jobs added (or lost) in the export sector averaged 460 and ranged from 50 to 1,020 in 1960. This relationship between the export and local sectors is relatively stable, and it is reasonable to believe that changes in the relationship may be explained in terms of upgrading of the export sector, import substitution, changes in the national parameters of demand and productivity in industries in the local sector, and changes in the size of the metropolitan market. The need to disaggregate national trends is clearly apparent from the finding that almost one-half of the job increases in metropolitan export activity during the 1950s were offset by job decreases in the same industry in other metropolitan areas. Just as important is the industrial dimension of employment change within metropolitan labor markets; three-fifths of the job increases in metropolitan export activity were offset by job decreases due to declining export activity in other industries in the same metropolis.

Growth of a metropolitan labor market must be viewed within the perspective of the larger regional or national urban system within which metropolitan areas compete for the location of industrial activity. Metropolitan growth implies a more intensive utilization of resources, an upgrading of the labor force, and a rise in wages and other business costs, including rents and taxes, which in turn affects the area's comparative advantage.

The findings suggest that as metropolitan places have grown, export industries characterized by low VAPE have been replaced by industries with higher VAPE. Concomitantly, the more labor-intensive (usually low-value-added, low-wage) industries have been attracted to low-cost areas with labor surpluses. At the same time, technological developments, such as the mechanization of agriculture, have given rise to labor surpluses in rural areas and created a labor market favorable to relocation. Construction of the interstate highway system improved the access of such areas to national markets, and the establishment of national power grids reduced regional differences in energy costs. Furthermore, the expanding industries are more footloose, and markets have shifted toward the warmer climates of the South and West. This push and pull of low-wage industries from high- to lower-cost areas is one of the basic processes occurring with economic growth.

Metropolitan areas may perhaps be best characterized as being in a continual state of dynamic disequilibrium, with the comparative advantages of each changing with its growth. The urban system develops as the national parameters change. The outcome of this developmental process, by which some functions are passed down and others up the urban hierarchy, is an upgrading of export activity in expanding metropolitan labor markets.

The general upgrading of metropolitan export activity, the increasing size of metropolitan labor markets, and changes in the national parameters, all tend to broaden the local sector and make the metropolis more self-sufficient. The process of import substitution and other developments that cause the trade multiplier to become larger are an increasing source of growth.

To summarize, there is a need for more sensitivity in national economic policy to spatial dimensions, that is, to the localized impact of swings in government spending or of changes in policy that influence the location of economic activity. There is also a need at the local level for assistance in understanding economic growth and change. The analytical framework used in this study serves both purposes, since the basic unit of analysis is the metropolitan labor market.

103

It is worth noting that, at the present time, regional analysis consists primarily of applying techniques developed for national aggregative analysis, such as input-output and econometric models, to states and multistate regions. These efforts are not likely to be very helpful for two reasons. First, the coefficients that must be specified are much more unstable in "open" subnational economies than in "closed" national economies, and hence data requirements are greater and results less satisfactory. Second, the regions examined are not functionally integrated economies, and hence the models do not simulate actual growth processes. The functional relationships within regional networks of urban places must be delineated before we formulate or implement national urban growth policies. We must understand the system on which we are operating. For example, a new town, satellite city, or growth center may be made to prosper, but its success may be at the expense of nearby established centers, which surrender vital activities to the new focus of activity (similar to suburban growth at the expense of the inner cities).

The task of analyzing metropolitan growth, though critical for effective metropolitan planning, is probably too great an undertaking for most metropolitan areas. The reason for this is, as noted above, that the metropolis is an "open" economy. Hence, effectively to analyze metropolitan growth, national and regional factors must be accounted for. Because of the present state of the art, the availability of qualified manpower, and the costs involved, this task cannot be performed satisfactorily at the local level. But the capability is required by many planning agencies such as the city halls, chambers of commerce, cooperative area-wide manpower planning systems (CAMPS), regional planning organizations, and so on and should therefore, be developed.

As we become more concerned with the spatial dimensions of economic growth, new issues will arise. We will want to determine what information or other services are required to improve the quality of location (or relocation) decisions and hence the over-all efficiency of the economy. Welfare implications will also have to be explored. Relocation does not necessarily imply a net gain to society. The optimal location decision accounts only for costs and benefits that are internalized by the decision-making unit over a particular time period. Should relocation be found to resemble a game of musical chairs where net externalized costs exceed net internalized benefits, then some form of intervention whereby some of the external costs are internalized may be justified. The spatial implications of changes in industrial organization should also be considered. Through a process of mergers and acquisitions, control of local firms is being given to large national and multinational corporations, thus decreasing the autonomy of local economies. This would suggest that local factors become less important in the location decision, as other corporate concerns are added. It is interesting to speculate about the effect of large corporations on the mobility of economic activity and on the national urban system. The larger the organization, the more perfect its information, the more aware it is of alternative opportunities, the more control it is likely to have over markets and prices, and the better able it is to finance a move (or close down a less profitable operation). Thus we may expect a greater "rationalization" of production and a concomitant increase in the relocation of activity. However, as the size of firm increases, the costs of relocation are likely to be increasingly

104

internalized (the more likely if the adversely affected operations are controlled by the same firm). This would reduce the attractiveness of relocation and decrease mobility. Increased size of corporations also suggests further separation of production and nonproduction (administrative) functions. Corporate headquarters will probably become increasingly concentrated in a few large nodal centers that can provide the wide range of services required. While nonproduction activities are passed up the hierarchy of cities, production facilities will be passed down as they become less dependent on the local business infrastructure. These are just a few of the issues we will want to explore as we increase our sensitivity to spatial dimensions.

Manpower Implications

Perhaps this study will contribute a new perspective from which to consider manpower problems arising from economic adjustment and structural change. In recent decades, national programs to assist local communities adversely affected by structural changes have grown rapidly. Of particular interest here are the numerous manpower programs, each developed in response to a perceived mismatch in the supply and demand for manpower in a particular segment of the labor market and each having a differential impact on local labor markets.* The growth in the scale and scope of federal intervention in local labor markets has, in effect, introduced a new dimension to federal economic policy that makes a new perspective necessary.

1. Manpower programs differ significantly from other economic policy measures. Unlike fiscal (taxation) and monetary policies, which implement national economic policy, manpower programs operate directly on local labor markets, not on national aggregates such as money supply, investment, and consumption. As a consequence, aggregate measures of economic activity, macro-models of the national economy, and theories pertaining to national economic growth are of limited use in the analysis of manpower problems. Moreover, manpower programs, while contributing to economic growth by increasing the supply of manpower and generally upgrading the labor force, do not stimulate aggregate demand sufficiently to increase aggregate employment.

The success of any manpower program depends primarily on whether jobs exist after the training ends. Thus, to succeed, the manpower effort must be appropriate to the type of development occurring in a local labor market—that is, training must be attuned to the needs of the localities with regard to expanding industries; since the type of change and adjustment problems must be approached within the context of the change and growth occurring in the

---

*Federal involvement in efforts to increase the employability of jobless and underemployed began under the Area Redevelopment Act of 1961 and was expanded by the Manpower Development and Training Act of 1962 and by the Economic Opportunity Act of 1964. Enrollment in the more than a dozen categorical grant programs is projected at 2.2 million during fiscal 1972 at a cost to the federal government of $3 billion.[2]

particular area. Both the methodology and findings of this study should prove useful to this purpose.

2. Not only does the manpower dimension require us to consider economic growth at a more disaggregated level, but it also demands that we take a more comprehensive view of the factors affecting the growth of local labor markets. Any development that has a significant impact on the location (or relocation) of economic activity will have implications for manpower policy. The impact of technological change, for example, must be viewed in terms of its effect on the location of economic activity as well as its over-all impact on industry productivity and employment. Similarly, trends in consumption patterns, in industrial organization, and in the geography of markets, including urbanization patterns and population shifts, affect the labor market inasmuch as they affect locations of economic activity.

There can be little doubt that government policies have an increasing impact on the location of economic activity and, hence, significant manpower implications. Competitive forces are strong, but changes in technology and corporate policies are conditioned by government policies. Moreover, the government has a very direct impact on urban growth patterns through investment in infrastructure, the location of its facilities, and the purchase of goods and services. The most striking example is, of course, the growth of the federal capital, Washington, D.C., which is almost solely attributable to the increased export of government services and associated activities. A military base at Key West, a defense aerospace contract, a space center in Huntsville, Strategic Air Command headquarters in Omaha, an Internal Revenue Service regional center in Andover, Massachusetts, a veterans' hospital in Denver, a federal court house, or a contract for motor vehicles, paper, or supplies—all have a significant impact on local labor markets and the urban system of which they are part.

Many other government programs and actions also have significant geographic impact. Various types of transfer payments, grants, tax incentives, mortgage policies, government reorganization, and subsidies have their effects concentrated in selected geographic areas. For example, mortgage subsidies stimulate construction employment in suburban areas; increased transfer payments stimulate local demand in consumer goods and services in areas where target populations (for example, the aged, welfare families) are concentrated. Moreover, policy changes made by regulatory commissions have significant impact on corporate policies concerning industrial organization, research and development, investment policies, location decision, and marketing strategies. For example, Federal Trade Commission policy with respect to mergers may hamper or facilitate the geographic concentration of employment in an industry; Interstate Commerce Commission rulings with respect to freight rates and route structures have similar implications. State and local government policies also enter the location equation and are weighted by firms and individuals alike. Industrial development programs or differentials in state corporate or personal income taxes may even sway a relocating firm to move across a state or county line, a move that may considerably affect the labor market.

Since manpower programs can only marginally increase the number of jobs and can reach only relatively small numbers of workers, the manpower

106

implications of other governmental actions must be recognized. It is even likely that other government programs and policies are more significant than the manpower programs themselves. Where the manpower implications of the policies of different government agencies are found to be in direct conflict, attempts could be made to resolve and coordinate them. While there is a general policy shift in this direction, greater initiative is required if manpower programs are to gain leverage.

Some steps have been made toward interagency evaluation and cooperation. The Environmental Protection Act of 1970 created a Council on Environmental Quality in the Executive Office of the President to review and monitor the effects of federal programs or programs that make use of federal funds or public land. An environmental statement must be made available to government officials and the public. Guidelines issued by the council state that the implications of the action for population distribution or concentration should be estimated and that alternative actions should be studied and developed. Will detailed guildlines require that the programs' impact on the labor market be considered? By executive order, the General Services Administration must now submit to the departments of Labor, Housing and Urban Development, Transportation and the Office of Economic Opportunity site proposals for new federal facilities to ensure that the objectives of each department will be considered.

Efforts to coordinate manpower programs both within the Department of Labor and with programs in other departments are restricted primarily to labor-surplus areas in depressed regions. Concentrated employment programs (CEPs), designed to marshal the full range of manpower and supportive services, have been established in many such areas. The Manpower Development and Training Act authorizes training programs linked to economic development in areas specified as redevelopment areas by the Department of Commerce under the Public Works and Economic Development Act. An even broader approach to coordination of manpower, educational, and economic development activities in rural areas is being sponsored jointly by the departments of Labor, Agriculture, and Health, Education, and Welfare.

The industrial and spatial dynamics of growth have important manpower implications. While trends in both industry productivity and expenditure patterns favor the growth of employment in metropolitan-type areas, they give rise to major imbalances in labor supply and social infrastructure in all types of areas as well as in individual labor markets. Adjustments among labor markets take time. A considerable lag occurred between employment declines in primary activities in non-metropolitan areas and the movement of low-productivity manufacturers to the areas with surplus manpower. Consequently, many rural (unskilled) workers continued to migrate to large (high-cost) urban centers even though jobs for unskilled workers were shifted out of the city and deficiencies in social infrastructure were becoming acute.

Employment prospects for the low-wage (particularly male) worker residing in the central city of metropolitan areas are not improving. Between 1960 and 1970, nonfarm employment increased slightly faster in non-metropolitan areas than in metropolitan areas, and a majority of the job increases in metropolitan areas went to residents outside the central city. If present trends persist and low-productivity export industries move out of the metropolis, local industries relocate in the suburbs, and the influx of unskilled workers into large metropolitan areas continues, imbalances in the labor market will be greatly aggravated. The issue will be whether it is industries or people that should be given assistance to move. Growth dynamics described in this study suggest that it makes more economic sense to help the people move to where economic activity is most viable. This implies either the building of low-income housing outside the central city or mobility assistance similar to the pilot programs being run in rural areas.

Another growth-related problem that has become more critical in recent years is the inability of some domestic industries to compete with foreign producers even when they shift to low-cost non-metropolitan areas. A program to aid workers displaced by imports was implemented in 1970, when the U.S. Tariff Commission made the initial determination under the Trade Adjustment Act of 1963, enabling the Department of Labor to certify for special employment assistance workers adversely affected by foreign imports.

The increased importance of geographical shift and industrial transition demonstrates the growing complexity of the adjustments that are occurring in regional and metropolitan labor markets as the national economy grows. As the pace and complexity of change increases, manpower information services and training and related programs will have to be more responsive to the growth process if they are to facilitate change and ensure that labor markets operate efficiently.

It is apparent that if we are to understand the problems that structural changes and urbanization create for both rural and urban areas, we need a conceptual framework that will take into account the spatial dimension of economic growth. As a nation, we have elected to draw up a national urban growth policy, yet we have devised no way to determine what our objectives should be or to evaluate alternative policies. The perspective of the national urban system developed here should be useful in this regard. There is obviously a great deal more that must be learned about systems of cities and metropolitan and regional development before we can piece together the mosaic of urban labor markets. It is hoped that in the interim the techniques developed and the analyses undertaken here will be useful.

NOTES

1. For an analysis of newly exporting places, see Richard V. Knight, "Employment Expansion and Metropolitan Trade" (unpublished dissertation, London School of Economics and Political Science, University of London, 1972), Table VI-6 and pp. 179-83.

2. See *Manpower Report of the President* (Washington, D.C., April 1971).

ABOUT THE AUTHOR

RICHARD VICTOR KNIGHT is Assistant Professor of Urban Economics,
Case Western Reserve University, and Senior Research Associate, Conservation
of Human Resources Project. He has been a part-time lecturer at New York
University, the City University of New York, and Columbia University and a
participant in The Jamaica Bay Environmental Impact Study Group, National
Academy of Sciences.

Dr. Knight has written the introductory chapter in *New York Is Very
Much Alive: A Manpower Perspective* (New York: McGraw-Hill, 1973). He has
also written *Jamaica Bay and Kennedy Airport: A Multidisciplinary Environmental Impact Study* (Washington, D.C.: National Academy of Sciences—
National Academy of Engineering, 1971) and has co-authored with Thomas M.
Stanback, Jr., *The Metropolitan Economy: The Process of Employment Expansion* (New York: Columbia University Press, 1970).

Dr. Knight received his Bachelor of Science Degree from Columbia University and his Ph.D. from London School of Economics and Political Science.

OTHER CONSERVATION OF HUMAN RESOURCES STUDIES— COLUMBIA UNIVERSITY

UNEMPLOYMENT IN THE URBAN CORE
An Analysis of Thirty Cities with Policy Recommendations

Stanley L. Friedlander, assisted by Robert Shick

THE LABOR MARKET: AN INFORMATION SYSTEM

Boris Yavitz, Dean W. Morse, with Anna B. Dutka

THE IMPACT OF FEDERAL ANTIPOVERTY POLICIES

Charles Brecher